Learning Through Movement and Music

Exercise Your Smarts

Debby Mitchell, EdD

GeoMotion
Move to Achieve

nan Kinetics

Library of Congress Cataloging-in-Publication Data

GeoMotion Group
  Learning through movement and music : exercise your smarts / GeoMotion Group, Inc.; Debby Mitchell, contributor.
     p. cm.
  Includes bibliographical references.
  ISBN-13: 978-1-4504-1299-5 (soft cover)
  ISBN-10: 1-4504-1299-8 (soft cover)
  1. Movement education. 2. Music in education. 3. Physical fitness for children. I. Mitchell, Debby. II. Title.
  GV452.G48 2011
  372.86'8--dc23
                              2011023277

ISBN-10: 1-4504-1299-8 (print)
ISBN-13: 978-1-4504-1299-5 (print)

All posters and lyrics courtesy of GeoMotion Group, Inc. Available: www.GeoMotiongroup.com.

All choreography created by Cammy Davis.

The web addresses cited in this text were current as of July 2011, unless otherwise noted.

Acquisitions Editor: Cheri Scott; **Developmental Editor:** Ragen E. Sanner; **Assistant Editor:** Anne Rumery; **Copyeditor:** Joanna Hatzopoulos; **Permissions Manager:** Dalene Reeder; **Graphic Designer:** Fred Starbird; **Graphic Artist:** Kathleen Boudreau-Fuoss; **Cover Designer:** Keith Blomberg; **DVD Face Designer:** Susan Rothermel Allen; **Photographer (cover):** © Human Kinetics and © GeoMotion Group, Inc.; **Photographer (interior):** p. 1, 6, 11, 28, 58, 63, 69, and 73, © Photodisc; p. 17 © 2001 RubberBall Productions; p. 36, 41 courtesy of GeoMotion Group, Inc. Available: http://www.GeoMotiongroup.com/product/exercise-your-smarts-8-pack-poster; all others © Human Kinetics unless otherwise noted.; **Art Manager:** Kelly Hendren; **Associate Art Manager:** Alan L. Wilborn; **Illustrations:** © Human Kinetics; **Printer:** United Graphics

The contents of this DVD are licensed for private home use and traditional, face-to-face classroom instruction only. For public performance licensing, please contact a sales representative at **www.HumanKinetics.com/SalesRepresentatives**.

Printed in the United States of America   10 9 8 7 6 5 4 3 2 1

Human Kinetics
Website: www.HumanKinetics.com

United States: Human Kinetics
P.O. Box 5076
Champaign, IL 61825-5076
800-747-4457
e-mail: humank@hkusa.com

Canada: Human Kinetics
475 Devonshire Road Unit 100
Windsor, ON N8Y 2L5
800-465-7301 (in Canada only)
e-mail: info@hkcanada.com

Europe: Human Kinetics
107 Bradford Road
Stanningley
Leeds LS28 6AT, United Kingdom
+44 (0) 113 255 5665
e-mail: hk@hkeurope.com

Australia: Human Kinetics
57A Price Avenue
Lower Mitcham, South Australia 5062
08 8372 0999
e-mail: info@hkaustralia.com

New Zealand: Human Kinetics
P.O. Box 80
Torrens Park, South Australia 5062
0800 222 062
e-mail: info@hknewzealand.com

Contents

Activity Finder and DVD-ROM Contents   v

Preface   vii

Introduction   ix

ACTIVITY **1** **Parts of an Exercise Bout** **1**

ACTIVITY **2** **Warm-Up** **6**

ACTIVITY **3** **Dynamic Stretch** **11**

ACTIVITY **4** **Where Are My Muscles?** **17**

ACTIVITY **5** **Muscle Workout** **21**

ACTIVITY **6** **Cardio March** **28**

ACTIVITY **7** **Cool-Down** **36**

ACTIVITY **8** **Static Stretch** **41**

ACTIVITY **9** **Interval Training** **48**

ACTIVITY **10** **Fitness Test** **53**

ACTIVITY **11** **I've Been Working on My Body** **58**
Components of Health-Related Fitness

ACTIVITY **12** **Boogie Woogie Bone Dance** **63**

ACTIVITY **13** **Why Do We Exercise?** **69**

ACTIVITY **14** **FITT Principle** **73**

References   79

About the Author   80

How to Use This DVD-ROM   81

Activity Finder and DVD-ROM Contents

Activity videos on DVD-ROM	Page in book	Description	Reproducibles on DVD-ROM
Activity 1— Parts of an Exercise Bout	1	Students learn the five parts of an exercise bout: warm-up, dynamic stretch, actual workout (for muscular strength and endurance and cardiovascular endurance), cool-down, and static stretch.	• Parts of an Exercise Bout poster • Parts of an Exercise Bout lyrics • Parts of an Exercise Bout Assessment 1 • Parts of an Exercise Bout Assessment 2 • Parts of an Exercise Bout Assessment 1 key • Parts of an Exercise Bout Assessment 2 key
Activity 2— Warm-Up	6	Students learn why and how to safely warm up the body and that they should warm up at a low intensity first in preparation for exercise.	• Warm-Up and Dynamic Stretch poster • Warm-Up lyrics • Warm-Up Assessment • Warm-Up Assessment key
Activity 3— Dynamic Stretch	11	Students learn why and how to safely perform a dynamic stretch and that it is an extension of the warm-up. The super six exercises are introduced to stretch the muscles and connective tissues at a joint.	• Warm-Up and Dynamic Stretch poster • Dynamic Stretch lyrics • Dynamic Stretch Assessment 1 • Dynamic Stretch Assessment 2 • Dynamic Stretch Assessment 2 key
Activity 4— Where Are My Muscles?	17	Students learn 13 muscle names and their locations: quadriceps, hamstrings, gluteus maximus, gastrocnemius, latissimus dorsi, erector spinae, rectus abdominis, obliques, pectoralis major, trapezius, biceps, triceps, and deltoid.	• Where Are My Muscles? poster • Where Are My Muscles? lyrics • Where Are My Muscles? Assessment • Where Are My Muscles? Assessment key
Activity 5— Muscle Workout	21	Students review the 13 muscles previously learned. In addition, they learn how a muscle works, definitions of repetition and set, and exercises to strengthen each muscle.	• Muscle Workout lyrics • Muscle Workout Assessment 1 • Muscle Workout Assessment 2 • Muscle Workout Assessment 1 key • Muscle Workout Assessment 2 key
Activity 6— Cardio March	28	Students learn about many cardio concepts: aerobics with oxygen, cardiovascular fitness, the talk test, using a scale of 1 to 10 for perceived exertion, what happens to breathing and heart rate during exercise, target heart rate zone, how and where to take a pulse, and the benefits of aerobic exercise.	• Perceived Exertion Method poster • Cardio March lyrics • Cardio March Assessment 1 • Cardio March Assessment 2 • Cardio March Assessment 1 key • Cardio March Assessment 2 key

(continued)

Activity videos on DVD-ROM	Page in book	Description	Reproducibles on DVD-ROM
Activity 7—Cool-Down	36	Students learn why and how to safely cool down the body and gradually let the body recover.	• Cool-Down and Static Stretch poster • Cool-Down lyrics • Cool-Down Assessment 1 • Cool-Down Assessment 2 • Cool-Down Assessment 1 key • Cool-Down Assessment 2 key
Activity 8—Static Stretch	41	Students learn why and how to safely perform a static stretch and that it is an extension of the cool-down. This is the best time to stretch the muscles that are still warm to increase flexibility and range of motion.	• Cool-Down and Static Stretch poster • Static Stretch lyrics • Static Stretch Assessment 1 • Static Stretch Assessment 2 • Static Stretch Assessment 1 key • Static Stretch Assessment 2 key
Activity 9—Interval Training	48	Students learn that interval training is alternating slow and fast intervals of exercise. Included is what occurs to breathing and heart rate.	• Interval Training lyrics • Interval Training Assessment 1 • Interval Training Assessment 2 • Interval Training Assessment 2 key
Activity 10—Fitness Test	53	Students perform a simple fitness test to the music. They try a sit-and-reach test for flexibility. Then, for 30 seconds each they try push-ups for muscular strength, do abdominal crunches for muscular endurance, and jump 4 corners for cardiovascular fitness.	• Fitness Test lyrics • Fitness Test Assessment 1 • Fitness Test Assessment 2 • Fitness Test Assessment 2 key
Activity 11—I've Been Working on My Body	58	Students learn about the components of fitness: flexibility, cardiovascular endurance, muscular strength and endurance, and body composition.	• Components of Health-Related Fitness poster • I've Been Working on My Body: Components of Fitness lyrics • I've Been Working on My Body Assessment 1 • I've Been Working on My Body Assessment 2 • I've Been Working on My Body Assessment 1 key • I've Been Working on My Body Assessment 2 key
Activity 12—Boogie Woogie Bone Dance	63	Students learn about major bones and where they are located in the body: cranium, mandible, vertebrae (cervical, thoracic, lumbar, sacrum, and coccyx), sternum, ribs, scapula, pelvis, radius, ulna, carpals, metacarpals, phalanges, femur, patella, tibia, fibula, talus, tarsals, and metatarsals.	• Bones poster • Boogie Woogie Bone Dance lyrics • Boogie Woogie Bone Dance Assessment 1 • Boogie Woogie Bone Dance Assessment 2 • Boogie Woogie Bone Dance Assessment 1 key • Boogie Woogie Bone Dance Assessment 2 key
Activity 13—Why Do We Exercise?	69	Students learn the variety of ways that exercise helps the body. Concepts include information about increasing energy, combating disease, strengthening the heart and lungs, improving circulation, speeding up messages from cell to cell, building better concentration, removing toxins, and many other health benefits.	• Why Do We Exercise? lyrics • Why Do We Exercise? Assessment 1 • Why Do We Exercise? Assessment 2 • Why Do We Exercise? Assessment 1 key • Why Do We Exercise? Assessment 2 key
Activity 14—FITT Principle	73	Students learn about the FITT principle: frequency, intensity, time, and type.	• FITT Principle poster • FITT Principle lyrics • FITT Principle Assessment • FITT Principle Assessment key

Preface

Learning Through Movement and Music: Exercise Your Smarts is a tool for physical education and classroom teachers to help students in third through seventh grade learn about the body, fitness, and health. This tool uses multisensory integration to enhance learning. Combining academic content, music, and movement encourages kinesthetic learning, which enlists more memory pathways for better recall of information.

The health and fitness curriculum focuses on 14 songs designed to educate students on how and why to exercise. While moving, students listen to educational lyrics about their bodies, their health, and how to improve their fitness. Debby Mitchell, EdD, developed the curriculum content and Maryann ("Mar") Harman provided her expertise by recording the lyrics to music.

The book provides the organizational structure for the learning content and includes thumbnails of the posters, handouts, and assessment pieces located on the DVD-ROM. These products help students synthesize the information from the book and lyrics through fill-in, true–false, multiple choice, and open-ended questions. To help facilitate their learning and use in the classroom, the lyrics themselves are also available on the DVD-ROM. This icon shows when items found on the DVD-ROM are being referenced.

Students can follow along with the video content on the *Learning Through Movement and Music: Exercise Your Smarts DVD-ROM*. A teacher and five students lead the activities in a fun and engaging way. Each section ends with open-ended closure questions for problem solving and to check comprehension. At any point during the closure, the classroom teacher may press Pause to get feedback from students.

You may notice the use of mats with numbers and directions on them used in some of the pictures in the book and posters and in the videos on the DVD-ROM. These are GeoMats, which aren't necessary to perform the movements described in this book but can come in handy. The chore-ography in the book is described without using a GeoMat, but GeoMat numbers are also provided from time to time when you might find them helpful for describing body positioning in space. To help you visualize the numbers and positions on a GeoMat, see figure 1.

Researchers are providing more insights into the importance of movement and cognition; thus, part of the title of the book is *Exercise Your Smarts*. The introduction provides more information about how the brain works and how the brain positively impacts learning. The introduction was coauthored by Jean Blaydes, who founded action-based learning, which puts brain-based learning into action with teacher-friendly, kid-tested, and kid-approved strategies that teach academic content kinesthetically. Finally, the brain research supports the need for physical activity.

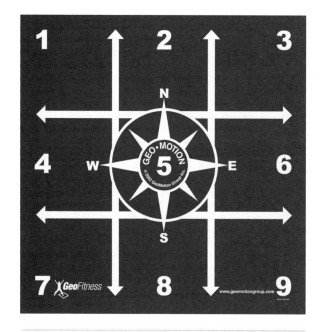

Figure 1 GeoMats aren't necessary to use the choreography in this book, but they can be useful because they provide a numbering system to describe space. See www.geomotiongroup.com for more information on GeoMats.

Photo courtesy of GeoMotion Group, Inc.

In addition to the introductory chapter about the brain, activities 1 through 8 educate students on the parts of an exercise bout: warm-up, dynamic stretch, learning about muscles, cardiovascular information, cool-down, and static stretch. The remaining activities provide information about why to exercise, the FITT principle, names of bones, interval training, and how and why to take a fitness test.

Combined with the rich content of the book, music and movement provide the base knowledge for a healthier life. Students can truly exercise their smarts!

Introduction

Jean Blaydes • Debby Mitchell

Why do we exercise? Some people exercise to lose weight. Others exercise to prevent disease. Some exercise just to feel better or to be healthy. One of the reasons we *should* exercise is for brain health.

Exercise benefits the brain even before it benefits the body. The brain does not store its own fuel, nor does it produce its own fuel. The brain relies on the body to get its needed fuel—oxygen and glucose—to the brain. The healthier and more physically fit the body is, the more efficiently the brain functions. This is because exercise changes the brain at a molecular level by

- growing new brain cells, a process called neurogenesis;
- producing BDNF (brain-derived neurotropic factor), nicknamed the fertilizer for the brain;
- strengthening secondary dendritic branching that increases memory retrieval; and
- improving mood by balancing the neurotransmitters endorphins, dopamine, cortisol, and serotonin.

The brain is a complex structure. More parts of the brain "light up," or are used, when a person is moving or physically active. See the figure, The Human Brain, on pages x and xi for some basic information on the anatomy of the brain.

HOW EXERCISE BENEFITS THE BRAIN

Exercise creates the optimal environment for neural plasticity, the ability of the brain to change. Exercise puts the brain and body into balance naturally by regulating brain chemicals that control mood and responses to stress. Research on the brain reveals how exercise can aid in learning and cognition (Ratey 2008):

Improved Brain Function (Medina 2008)

- Increased capacity for learning with the growth of an estimated 9,000 cells (neurons) daily
- Increased neurons in the hippocampus, the learning and memory center of the brain
- Protection of the brain functions for increased health
- Increased connections among existing neural pathways
- Increased brain organization and integration

Enhanced Cognition (Etnier 1997)

- Enhanced mental performance, memory, learning, attention, decision making, and multitasking
- Increased adaptivity, efficiency, and ability to reorganize neural pathways based on new experiences
- Increased executive function to enhance higher-level mental skills that inhibit impulses, shift focus, control emotions, initiate, plan, organize, and monitor
- Improved arousal and vigilance that in educational terms translates to focus
- Improved perception
- Improved cellular function (learning translates from short-term to long-term memory and learning becomes automatic)
- Decreased distraction
- Improved process of putting thought into action
- Improved ability to put patterns into sequences (letters into words, words into sentences).

THE HUMAN BRAIN

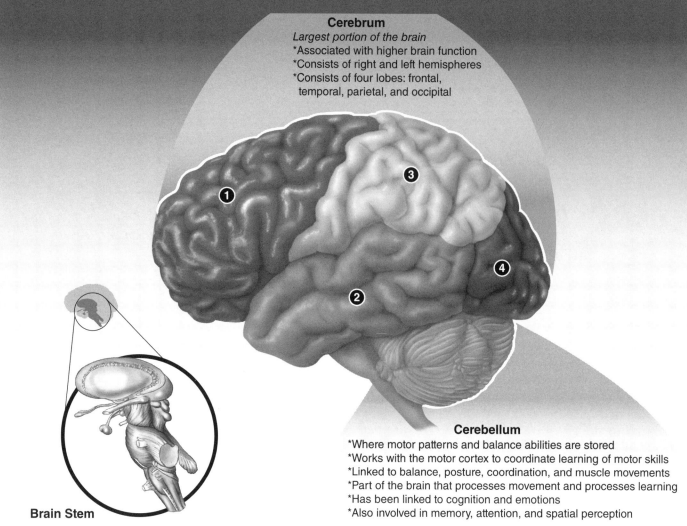

Cerebrum
Largest portion of the brain
*Associated with higher brain function
*Consists of right and left hemispheres
*Consists of four lobes: frontal, temporal, parietal, and occipital

Cerebellum
*Where motor patterns and balance abilities are stored
*Works with the motor cortex to coordinate learning of motor skills
*Linked to balance, posture, coordination, and muscle movements
*Part of the brain that processes movement and processes learning
*Has been linked to cognition and emotions
*Also involved in memory, attention, and spatial perception

Brain Stem
*Survival mechanism of the brain
*Automatic processes happen, such as heartbeat, respiration, sleep, and alertness

Areas of the Cerebrum

❶ Frontal Lobe
*The "library" of the brain where information is stored
*Deals with planning and thinking

❷ Temporal Lobe
*Recognition of sounds, music, faces, and objects
*Where language and hearing are processed

❸ Parietal Lobe
*Deals with reception of sensory information from the opposite (contralateral) side of body
*Plays a part in reading, writing, language, and circulation
*Where senses are deciphered and where problem solving takes place

❹ Occipital Lobe
*Where vision is processed
*The "movie screen" of the brain

Motor Cortex and Corpus Callosum

The motor cortex and the corpus callosum divide the brain into four quadrants.
All four quadrants (both sides and front and back) need to communicate for optimal learning to occur.

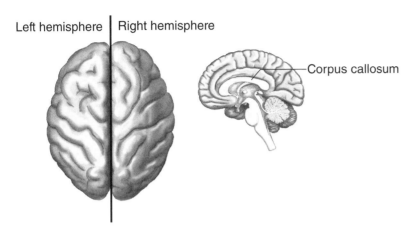

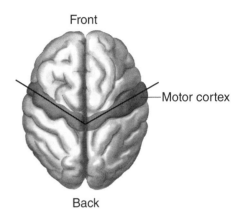

The corpus callosum divides the
brain into the right and left hemispheres.

The motor cortex divides
the brain from front to back.

Additional Areas of the Brain and Nervous System Aided by Exercise

Neurons
*Nerve cells that can receive, process, and transmit signals
*Tiny information-processing units with thousands of connections
*Each consists of a cell body and two types of projections: the dendrites and an axon

Limbic System
Not a structure but a series of nerve pathways incorporating structures deep within the temporal lobes:

Thalamus
*Transfers incoming sensory information to other parts of the brain
*Key sensory relay station for all senses except smell

Hypothalamus
*Controls release of hormones and moderates numerous bodily functions
*Influences and regulates appetite, hormone secretion, digestion, circulation, emotions, and sleep

Hippocampus
*Consolidates learning
*Strongly involved in learning and memory formation

Amygdala
*Emotional component of long-term memory
*Part of the critical processing area for the senses and plays a critical role in learning, cognition, and processing of emotional memories

Reprinted, by permission, from L. Kenney, J. Wilmore, and D. Costill, 2012, *Physiology of sport and exercise*, 5th ed. (Champaign, IL: Human Kinetics), 78.

Improved Memory

- Enhanced short-term working memory and increased long-term potentiality
- Physiological strengthening of the brain as the result of dendritic branching
- Staved-off symptoms and signs of dementia

Reduced Stress

- Reduced test anxiety
- Decreased symptoms of depression after just three days of exercise
- Improved adaptation to challenges in a changing environment
- Decreased toxic effects of high levels of stress
- Reduced neuronal death caused by chronic stress

Balanced Mood and Behavior

- Improved attention, motivation, self-esteem, cooperation
- Ameliorated learned helplessness
- Improved resilience and self-confidence
- Increased ability to withstand stress and frustration
- Fewer behavior problems
- Increased coping skills when presented with a new situation
- Increased self-discipline and self-esteem
- Reduction or elimination of the need for ADHD medications and antidepressants
- Regulated mood through the natural balance of neurotransmitters
- Regulated sleep patterns for increased alertness during school hours
- Intrinsic sense of reward, motivation, and satisfaction
- Impulse control
- Joyful attitude
- Increased state of happiness and life satisfaction

Improved Social Skills and Behavior

- Lower levels of drug use in teens
- Better family relationships
- Noticeable improvement in key personal, social, cooperative, and communication skills
- Improved attention, impulsivity, motivation, self-esteem, and cooperation

Improved Academic Performance (Dwyer et al. 2001)

- Improved reading and math scores
- Improved reading comprehension and analysis
- Higher IQ scores
- Higher grade-point average in adolescents
- Enhanced creativity
- Intensified focus in classroom
- Improved problem-solving skills
- Reduced truancy and dropout rates

HEALTH AND LEARNING

Healthy, active kids make better learners. We are not designed to sit. We are designed to move. Dr. John Medina, author of *Brain Rules* (2008), says this in his July 5, 2011, blog: "The human brain appears to have been designed to solve problems related to surviving in an outdoor setting in unstable meteorological conditions and to do so in near constant motion. So, if you wanted to design a learning environment that was directly opposed to what the brain is naturally good at doing, you'd design a frickin' classroom!"

A new study from American Cancer Society (2011) finds it's not just how much physical activity you get but how much time you spend sitting that can affect your risk of premature death. Time spent sitting is independently associated with total mortality, regardless of physical activity level. Public health messages should promote being physically active as well as reducing sedentary time.

A 2009 study by Hillman and colleagues shows that a single bout of moderate exercise is beneficial for cognitive function. Students walked for 20 minutes on a treadmill before doing a cognitive task; they were compared to students sitting and doing a cognitive task. The conclusion was a positive outcome linking physical activity, attention, and academic achievement. Cumulative brain scans of the participants (see figure I.1) illustrate that the active brain is better prepared to learn.

The 2009 Texas Youth Fitness Study conducted by the Cooper Institute compared Fitnessgram fitness scores to scores from a standardized test called TAKS (Texas Assessment of Knowledge and Skills). The researchers found significant associations between physical fitness and indicators of academic achievement:

- Academic performance. Higher levels of fitness are associated with better academic performance.
- School attendance. Higher levels of fitness are associated with better school attendance.
- School incidents. Higher levels of fitness are associated with fewer negative incidents at school.

MOVING WITH INTENTION AND LEARNING

Movement with intention anchors learning and prepares the brain for learning (Blaydes 2000). Neuroscience supports the link of exercise, physical activity, and movement to improved academic performance. A 2011 study by the American Academy of Pediatrics shows that intentional movement and exercise can improve test scores. The study adds to growing evidence that exercise is good not only for the body but also for the mind. In the study, first- and second-graders moved through stations in the action-based learning lab, learning developmentally appropriate movement skills while basic academic skills were reinforced. For example, children traced shapes on the ground while sitting on scooters and walked on ladders while naming colors on each rung or reciting sight words.

Third- through sixth-graders had access to exercise equipment with TV monitors with math problems playing for review. For instance, a treadmill had a monitor that played geography lessons as a student ran through the scene, and a rock-climbing wall was outfitted with numbers that changed as the students climbed so that they could work on math skills. The results of the study showed that the time spent out of a traditional classroom in order to increase physical education did not hurt students' academic achievement. In fact, students' test scores improved. Specifically, the number of students reaching their goals on the state tests increased from 55 percent before the program was initiated to 68.5 percent after the program was initiated. When carefully designed physical education programs are implemented, children's academic achievement does not suffer.

The action-based learning lab described in the 2011 study is an example of how intentional movement prepares the brain for learning, each station having a link to learning. The brain and body's movement and learning systems are interdependent and interactive (Madigan 2006). For example, motor development provides the framework that the brain uses for sequencing

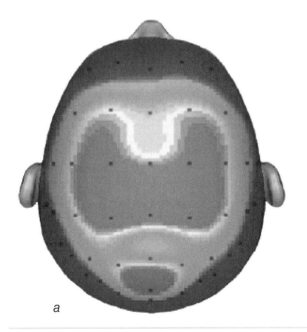 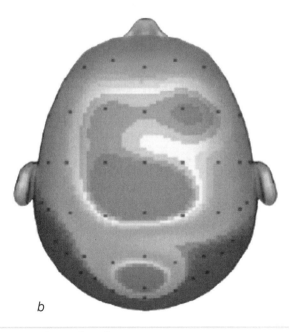

a   b

Figure I.1 *(a)* Brain scan of participants after sitting and *(b)* brain scan after walking for 20 minutes.

Reprinted from *Neuroscience*, Vol. 159, C.H. Hillman et al., "The effect of acute treadmill walking on cognitive control and academic achievement in preadolescent children," pgs. 1044-1054, Copyright 2009, with permission from Elsevier.

the patterns needed for academic concepts. The body's vestibular system controls balance and spatial awareness and facilitates a student's ability to place words and letters on a page. When a child walks or crawls in specific patterns, the brain's ability to encode symbols is enhanced and the four visual fields needed for eye tracking are strengthened. Proper development, enrichment, and remediation of these systems are critical to a child's ability to learn.

Movement, physical activity, and rhythmic patterns enhance learning and understanding. Students use gestures, actions, movement patterns, songs, and dance to understand academic concepts and anchor learning. The concept is called embodied cognition. When more modalities are used in learning a concept, the information is stored in several areas of the brain so the brain has more memory pathways for retrieving the information.

The lessons in this book and DVD-ROM address movement, physical activity, and rhythmic patterns that will help students learn and remember information about health and physical activity. For example, in activity 1, the song "Parts of an Exercise Bout" teaches students about the importance of preparing the body for a workout, completing the workout, and relaxing the body after a workout, or bout of exercise. Students learn movements that go with each part (warm-up, static stretch, workout, cool-down, and dynamic stretch) that provide physical activity and rhythmic patterns set to music, which students repeat throughout the song to aid memory. After the song and movements are over, questions on the DVD reinforce what students have learned. You can use the assessments to determine how well students remember the information once the song and movement session are complete. An example is a lesson from *Thinking on Your Feet* (2000) by Jean Blaydes Madigan:

Action Punctuation

Read a sentence or story. Punctuate using the following body movements and sounds.

- Capital letter—jump up and say, "Go."
- Period—Put your fist on your nose and say, "Whoa."
- Comma—Put your hands on your hips, circle hips around, and say, "Slow down."
- Question mark—Shrug shoulders with hands up in air and say, "Huh?"
- Exclamation mark—Grab the air with the right fist and bring down forcefully and say, "Yes."
- Quotation marks—Pretend to make quotation marks in the air with fingers and say, "Ching, ching."
- Apostrophe—Use the elbow to make an apostrophe in the air and say, "Not."

Reprinted, by permission, from J.B. Madigan, 2000, *Thinking on your feet* (Murphy, TX: Action Based Learning).

SUMMARY

We can exercise our smarts by exercising to be smart. Healthy, active students make better learners. In fact, healthy, active people of any age make better learners. Our bodies are designed for exercise. As stated previously, exercise benefits the brain first. We exercise to help our brains work better and learn better. The brain is only as healthy as the body that carries it. When we take care of our bodies, we take care of our brains.

PARTS OF AN EXERCISE BOUT

Physical exercise is activity performed in order to develop or maintain fitness and overall health. Typically exercise is a planned and structured activity for the purpose of conditioning a part or all of the body. The workout or training session (also called an exercise bout) should be safe, with a planned sequence of activities. The sequence begins with parts 1 and 2 (warm-up and dynamic stretch), which prepare the body for exercise. Part 3 is the workout, and parts 4 and 5 (cool-down and static stretch) aid in recovery from exercise. The different parts in an exercise bout ensure proper progression for an individual to exercise safely, avoid injuries, and increase health benefits of exercise. The parts are as follows:

1. **Warm-up**—The goal of the warm-up is to prepare the body for physical work and takes approximately 3 to 5 minutes. The purpose is to increase blood circulation and to warm up muscles. The warm-up includes activities such as jogging, marching, and other low-intensity exercises.

2. **Dynamic stretch**—The goal of the dynamic stretch is to help prevent injury by ensuring that muscles and connective tissues at joints are prepared for exercise. The purpose is to work the different joint areas actively with exercises that use a full range of motion. The dynamic stretch takes approximately 3 to 5 minutes and should be gentle and controlled.

3. **The workout**—The workout is the main goal of the entire exercise bout. Most workouts have the specific purpose of working to improve cardiovascular (heart) or muscular strength or endurance (muscles). Some workouts include only heart or other muscles. Many workouts include both.

    • **Cardiovascular**—To improve cardiovascular fitness a person needs to keep moving continuously for 20 to 60 minutes. An individual needs to work out moderately to vigorously to get a quality workout.

    • **Muscular strength or endurance**—The workout may include a focus on working particular muscles to make them stronger. This may include push-ups, curl-ups, weightlifting, or other muscle-specific exercises.

PARTS OF AN EXERCISE BOUT

PREPARATION

PART 1
Warm-Up
3–5 Minutes
- Increases blood flow
- Warms up muscles

PART 2
Dynamic Stretch
3–5 Minutes
- Active stretching
- Warms muscles and connective tissues
- Helps prevent injury

WORKOUT

PART 3
Workout
20–60 Minutes
- Cardiovascular (heart) workout
- Muscular endurance or strength (muscle) workout

RECOVERY

PART 4
Cool-Down
3–5 Minutes
- Slows down heart rate and breathing

PART 5
Static Stretch
3–5 Minutes
- Stretches and lengthens muscles and connective tissues
- Improves flexibility

PART 1 / PART 2:
- Low-intensity exercise
- Walking
- Jogging
- Swimming
- Biking
- Jumping rope

- Low-intensity exercise
- Full range of motion
- Exercises for each joint to lengthen and stretch muscles

PART 3:
- Cardio – Moderate to vigorous aerobic (continuous) activity
- Muscle – Work each muscle group including: *back, arms, shoulders, neck, abdominals, and legs*

PART 4 / PART 5:
- Low-intensity exercise similar to warm-up but even slower

- Stretch for each muscle and joint area
- Hold each stretch for 20 seconds or more

This poster, found on the DVD-ROM, is a fun visual to use in the classroom to help students remember the five parts of an exercise bout.

4. **Cool-down**—After the workout, heart rate and breathing are elevated. The goal of the cool-down is to allow the body to slow down and recover from exercise. To achieve the cool-down an individual slows down movement to a low intensity for 3 to 5 minutes. The heart rate should get lower and breathing should return to normal.

5. **Static stretch**—The goal of the static stretch is to stretch the muscles and connective tissues to improve flexibility. The purpose is to try and stretch at each major joint of the body and hold the stretch to allow time for the muscle to lengthen. Each stretch should be held at least 20 seconds and maybe even longer. The static stretch session should last 3 to 5 minutes.

Lyrics and Actions to "Parts of an Exercise Bout"

Lyrics	Actions
Introduction and Chorus:	
E, to the X, to the E, to the R to the C—I—S—E	Jump in place, then jump to the right with a hitchhiking motion; jump left, then left again with a hitchhiking motion; jump right, then right again with a hitchhiking motion. (If using a GeoMat, jump 5, 6, 5, 4, 5, and back to 6.) Perform hand and arm waves.
E, to the X, to the E, to the R to the C—I—S—E	Jump left, then left again with a hitchhiking motion; jump to the right, then right again witha hitchhiking motion; jump left, then left again with a hitchhiking motion. (If using GeoMat, jump 5, 4, 5, 6, 5, and back to 4.) Perform hand and arm waves.
Exercise	
Verse 1:	
An exercise bout—has five parts	Do a wide march, hold up five fingers. (If using a GeoMat, march on 4 and 6.)
Get to know them—exercise your smarts	Do a narrow march, point to your head (brain) to show you are smart. (If using a GeoMat, march on 5.)
One's the warm-up—exercise gingerly	Do a slow knee lift motion.
Two's a dynamic stretch—helps prevent injury	Alternately reach the arms up above the head and return (for several repetitions).
Three's the workout, it's all about this part	Continue reaches.
For muscles, strength;	Show your muscles (flex the biceps).
for cardio, heart	Place both hands over the heart (to show beating).
Four's the cool-down—bring your heart rate low	Move the hands from high to low, then stand tall.
Five's the static stretch—flexibility will grow	Perform a shoulder stretch and hold.
Repeat Chorus.	
Verse 2:	
Let's see if you remember—let's review	Point to your head (brain) while doing a wide march.
Act out each step—we'll watch what you do	Do a narrow march.
One's the warm-up—exercise gingerly	Do a slow knee lift motion.

(continued)

Lyrics	Actions
Two's a dynamic stretch—helps prevent injury	Alternately reach the arms up above the head and return (for several repetitions).
Three's the workout, it's all about this part	Continue reaches.
For muscles, strength;	Show your muscles (flex the biceps).
for cardio, heart	Place both hands over the heart (to show beating).
Four's the cool-down—bring your heart rate low	Move the hands from high to low, then stand tall.
Five's the static stretch—flexibility will grow	Perform a shoulder stretch and hold.
Repeat Chorus.	
Verse 3:	
Jump to the right—show me again	Jump a quarter-turn to the right. (If using a GeoMat, face east.)
Keep the info in your brain—do it with a friend	Point to your head (brain).
One's the warm-up—exercise gingerly	Do a slow knee lift motion.
Two's a dynamic stretch—helps prevent injury	Alternately reach the arms up above the head and return (for several repetitions).
Three's the workout, it's all about this part	Continue reaches.
For muscles, strength;	Show your muscles (flex the biceps).
for cardio, heart	Place both hands over the heart (to show beating).
Four's the cool-down—bring your heart rate low	Move the hands from high to low, then stand tall.
Five's the static stretch—flexibility will grow	Perform a shoulder stretch and hold.
Repeat Chorus.	
Verse 4:	
Jump 180 degrees for fun	Jump halfway around. (If using a GeoMat, face west.)
Do it one more time—this song's not done	Hold up the index finger.
One's the warm-up—exercise gingerly	Do a slow knee lift motion.
Two's a dynamic stretch—helps prevent injury	Alternately reach the arms up above the head and return (for several repetitions).
Three's the workout, it's all about this part	Continue reaches.
For muscles, strength;	Show your muscles (flex the biceps).
for cardio, heart	Place both hands over the heart (to show beating).
Four's the cool-down—bring your heart rate low	Move the hands from high to low, then stand tall.
Five's the static stretch—flexibility will grow	Perform a shoulder stretch and hold.
Repeat Chorus.	Jump with hitchhiking motions and hand waves. Face the front for the ending. (If using a GeoMat, face north.)

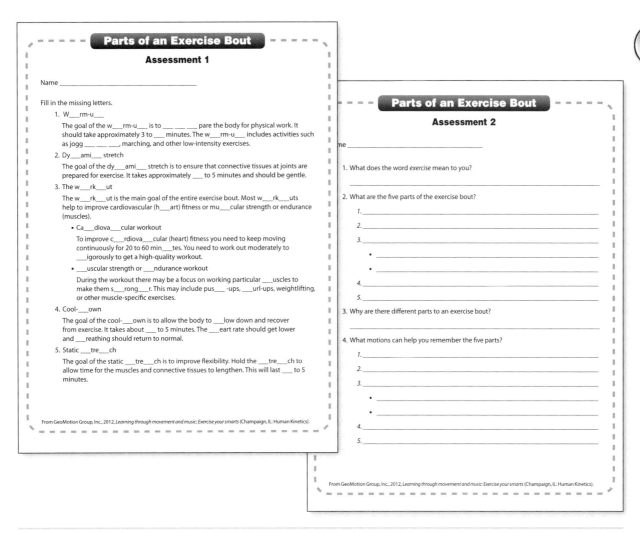

Parts of an Exercise Bout

Assessment 1

Name _____

Fill in the missing letters.

1. W___rm-u___

   The goal of the w___rm-u___ is to ___ ___ ___ pare the body for physical work. It should take approximately 3 to ___ minutes. The w___rm-u___ includes activities such as jogg ___ ___ ___, marching, and other low-intensity exercises.

2. Dy___ami___ stretch

   The goal of the dy___ami___ stretch is to ensure that connective tissues at joints are prepared for exercise. It takes approximately ___ to 5 minutes and should be gentle.

3. The w___rk___ut

   The w___rk___ut is the main goal of the entire exercise bout. Most w___rk___uts help to improve cardiovascular (h___art) fitness or mu___cular strength or endurance (muscles).

   • Ca___diova___cular workout

     To improve c___rdiova___cular (heart) fitness you need to keep moving continuously for 20 to 60 min___tes. You need to work out moderately to ___igorously to get a high-quality workout.

   • ___uscular strength or ___ndurance workout

     During the workout there may be a focus on working particular ___uscles to make them s___rong___r. This may include pus___ -ups, ___url-ups, weightlifting, or other muscle-specific exercises.

4. Cool-___own

   The goal of the cool-___own is to allow the body to ___low down and recover from exercise. It takes about ___ to 5 minutes. The ___eart rate should get lower and ___reathing should return to normal.

5. Static ___tre___ch

   The goal of the static ___tre___ch is to improve flexibility. Hold the ___tre___ch to allow time for the muscles and connective tissues to lengthen. This will last ___ to 5 minutes.

From GeoMotion Group, Inc., 2012, *Learning through movement and music: Exercise your smarts* (Champaign, IL: Human Kinetics).

Parts of an Exercise Bout

Assessment 2

Name _____

1. What does the word *exercise* mean to you?

   _____

2. What are the five parts of the exercise bout?

   1. _____

   2. _____

   3. _____

      • _____

      • _____

   4. _____

   5. _____

3. Why are there different parts to an exercise bout?

   _____

4. What motions can help you remember the five parts?

   1. _____

   2. _____

   3. _____

      • _____

      • _____

   4. _____

   5. _____

From GeoMotion Group, Inc., 2012, *Learning through movement and music: Exercise your smarts* (Champaign, IL: Human Kinetics).

Parts of an Exercise Bout handouts and answer keys are available on the DVD-ROM.

ACTIVITY 2

WARM-UP

The goal of the warm-up is to prepare the body for physical work. The warm-up should include low-intensity movements for approximately 3 to 5 minutes. This allows the blood to circulate through the body and gives the muscles time to get warm. The warm-up increases blood flow to the muscles, tendons, and ligaments so that they are ready for moderate to vigorous activity. When muscles are warm, they are less likely to be injured.

What does low-intensity mean? It means starting off slow and gradually building up. It is similar to starting a car engine. When a car is first started, the motor needs to run before someone pushes too hard on the accelerator. An individual should gently press the accelerator and gradually speed up to help get gas moving through the engine and provide oil to all the working parts of the car. Once the car is warm, an individual can accelerate faster without damage to the car.

As with a car, an individual should start working out the body slowly, then gradually increase effort to allow blood to circulate to all parts of the body and the muscles to get warm. This ensures that the body is prepared for more vigorous work without injury. To warm up the body, a person starts with a walk, a slow jog, or another type of low-intensity activity.

An individual needs to work different muscles, so it is good to have a variety of exercises that move the body in different ways. Some other exercises might include jumping jacks, jumping rope, and knee lifts.

Remember, the purpose is to increase blood circulation and to warm up muscles. A person can usually tell the warm-up is occurring because breathing becomes a little faster and the heart beats a little faster. Often perspiration occurs; it is another sign that the muscles are getting warm.

The reason that a person needs to warm up for at least 3 minutes is that it takes that long to get the blood circulated to all the muscles of the body and warm them up. They need to be warm to be ready to go to the next part of the exercise bout, which is the dynamic stretch.

WARM-UP AND DYNAMIC STRETCH

GeoFitness

WARM-UP — PREPARES THE BODY TO WORK OUT

★ Purpose: *Low-intensity activities to warm up the muscles and get blood circulating throughout the entire body.*

★ Jogging ★ Knee lifts ★ Step touches ★ Squats ★ Jumping rope ★ Jumping jacks

DYNAMIC STRETCH — ACTIVELY STRETCHES AND WARMS MUSCLES AND JOINTS

★ Purpose: *Stretches the muscles and loosens or stretches the connective tissues at joints to help prevent injury.*

STRAIGHT-LEG MARCH	TAP BEHIND	HAND WALKS	TORSO TWISTS	ARM CIRCLES	HEEL RAISES
• Stand up straight. • Gently lift one straight leg out in front. • Repeat with other leg. • Reach with opposite arm. • Continue to alternate leg lifts.	• Start in standing position. • Tap your foot or toe diagonally behind you. • Rotate arms and reach like you are skating. • Continue to alternate legs.	• Start in standing position. • Stretch and place hands on the floor. • Walk hands forward until in push-up position. • Walk hands back. • Repeat.	• Start in standing position. • Bend knees into a slight squat while keeping back straight. • Keep the hips and lower body still and twist the upper body or torso from side to side.	• Can be performed in standing or sitting position. • Circle arms forward then backward *(slowly and with control)*.	• Start in standing position. • Lift heels off the floor. • Slowly lower them back down. • Repeat.
• Stretches: *hip and lower back area, arms, upper back, and shoulders*	• Stretches: *front of the thigh, hip, knee, ankle areas, back and sides (torso or core), shoulders, and arms*	• Stretches: *shoulders, back, neck, arms, wrists, hips, legs, and ankles*	• Stretches: *torso (or core), which is between shoulders and hips*	• Stretches: *shoulders*	• Stretches: *ankles and back of the calves, called the gastrocnemius (or gastroc)*

Exercise Your Smarts
GeoMotion Group, Inc. © 2010
www.geomotiongroup.com

GeoMotion Move to Achieve

This poster, found on the DVD-ROM, can help students remember moves to warm up and to dynamically stretch their muscles.

Lyrics and Actions to "Warm-Up"

Lyrics	Actions
Introduction	
(Music plays and "warm-up" is whispered.)	Do alternating heel lifts.
Chorus 1:	
I'm warming up—warming up—getting warm	Do alternating knee lifts.
I'm warming up—I'm warming up—so I can perform	
Warming up—warming up—getting warm	
Warming up—warming up—so I can perform	
Verse 1:	
Get ready to exercise—get your muscles warm	Perform a triangle (V) step: left foot steps forward wide, then right foot steps forward wide, left foot steps back narrow, right foot steps back narrow, feet end up together. (If using a GeoMat, step on 1,3,5,5.)
Before you work out—then you'll do no harm	
Nice and slow is the way to start	
I know you'll do it—'cause you're smart	
Verse 2:	
Try a jog—keep it nice and slow	
Muscles will have increased blood flow	Jog slowly: 1 step for every 2 beats of music.
Jog a little faster—keep a steady pace	Jog a little faster: 1 step per beat of music.
Swing your arms—but it's not a race	Provide more arm movement in the swinging motion of the run.
Verse 3:	
Try knee lifts—but not too high	Do alternate knee lifts (every 2 beats).
Lift them up—toward the sky	
Move your arms—warm them too	Move the arms and touch the knees: right hand to left knee and left hand to right knee.
Touch your knees—right on cue	
Chorus 2:	
I'm warming up—I'm warming up—I'm getting warm	Do alternating heel lifts.
I'm warming up—I'm warming up—so I can perform	
I'm warming up—I'm warming up—I'm getting warm	Do alternating knee lifts.
I'm warming up—I'm warming up—so I can perform	
Verse 4:	
Step side to side—left and right	Alternate step taps: Step left and tap right foot; step right and tap left foot; repeat. (If using a GeoMat: Step on 4 with the left foot, tap the right toe on 4, step to 6 with the right foot, tap 6 with the left toe.)
Tap your toes—keep abdominals tight	

Lyrics	Actions
Rotate torso—from east and west	Stand with feet wide apart and begin reaching right (east) and left (west) across the body. (If using a GeoMat, keep the feet on 6 and 4.)
Keep warming up—do your best	
Verse 5:	
Legs in straddle—legs stay wide	Legs stay wide with the knees bent to be in a squat position.
Bend and straighten—shift side to side	Shift squat position side to side; make sure the knees are not past toes in the squat position.
Bob and weave—keep your hands in front	While moving side to side, also move up and down as a boxer with the hands in front for protection.
Squat even lower—try this boxing stunt	Move even lower in the squat position.
Verse 6:	
Pretend to jump rope—jump double	Pretend to jump rope with a double jump to the beat of the music.
Show your pride—you'll have no trouble	
Jump a little higher—leave the ground	Jump higher while still jumping to the beat of the music.
Move your feet—hear that sound	
Verse 7:	
Try a jumping jack—wide and together	Perform a slow jumping jack so that feet are out wide and then together to the timing of the lyrics. (If using a GeoMat, jump on 4 and 6, then jump with both feet on 5.)
Make your landing—light as a feather	
Coordinate your arms—up and down	Arms are in time with feet and music.
Smile the whole time—please don't frown	
Verse 8:	
You got started with great form	
Now your muscles are nice and warm	
Bet you know what comes next	
You're all ready for a dynamic stretch	Do alternating knee lifts.
Ending:	
Stretch it, stretch it	Do diagonal arms (one goes up while the other down) 2 times.
Get ready to stretch it	Do biceps curls.
Stretch it, stretch it	Do diagonal arms (one goes up while the other down) 2 times.
Get ready to stretch it	Do biceps curls.
Stretch it, stretch it	Do diagonal arms.

(continued)

Lyrics and Actions to "Warm Up" *(continued)*

Lyrics	Actions
Get ready to stretch it	Do biceps curls.
Stretch it, stretch it	Do diagonal arms.
Get ready to stretch it	Do biceps curls.
(Music is played and "You're warm" is whispered.)	Do heel lifts, marching knee lifts, and show biceps muscles.

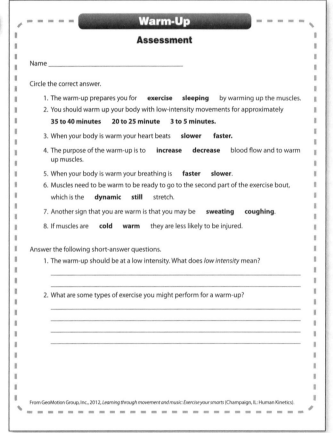

Warm-Up

Assessment

Name _____

Circle the correct answer.

1. The warm-up prepares you for **exercise** **sleeping** by warming up the muscles.
2. You should warm up your body with low-intensity movements for approximately **35 to 40 minutes** **20 to 25 minute** **3 to 5 minutes.**
3. When your body is warm your heart beats **slower** **faster.**
4. The purpose of the warm-up is to **increase** **decrease** blood flow and to warm up muscles.
5. When your body is warm your breathing is **faster** **slower**.
6. Muscles need to be warm to be ready to go to the second part of the exercise bout, which is the **dynamic** **still** stretch.
7. Another sign that you are warm is that you may be **sweating** **coughing**.
8. If muscles are **cold** **warm** they are less likely to be injured.

Answer the following short-answer questions.

1. The warm-up should be at a low intensity. What does *low intensity* mean?

_____
_____

2. What are some types of exercise you might perform for a warm-up?

_____
_____
_____
_____

From GeoMotion Group, Inc., 2012, *Learning through movement and music: Exercise your smarts* (Champaign, IL: Human Kinetics).

The Warm-Up handout and answer key are available on the DVD-ROM.

DYNAMIC STRETCH

The dynamic stretch is an extension of the warm-up. Once the warm-up has been performed for 3 to 5 minutes and the muscles are warm, the dynamic stretch is then performed for an additional 3 to 5 minutes. The combination of increased blood flow from the warm-up and elasticity from the dynamic stretch helps keep the body safe during exercise because warm, flexible muscles and tissues are less likely to be injured during a workout.

Therefore, the purpose of the dynamic stretch is to continue to stretch the muscles and to loosen or stretch the connective tissues at a joint. This step prepares the body for the workout and decreases chances for injury.

A joint is where two or more bones come together, such as in the neck, shoulders, elbows, wrists, fingers, back, hips, knees, ankles, and toes. The connective tissues that connect muscles to bone or bone to bone need to be warm and stretched to help a person exercise safely.

During the dynamic stretch an individual should move as many of the joint areas as possible in a slow, controlled manner to allow the connective tissue to stretch. Think of a piece of candy, such as taffy: If a person does not get it warm and pulls it too fast, it tears into two pieces. If an individual gets it warm and pulls gently, it stretches.

Remember that *dynamic* means moving. In other words, a person is slowly moving to stretch the body. It is not a still or held stretch (static). Perform slow, controlled stretches at the different joint areas. For the dynamic stretch an individual should move the joint area and stretch in a full range of motion. For example, if a person wanted to stretch out the shoulders, they would stretch the arms up, behind, down low, and in front of the body to stretch the shoulder in as many positions as possible. Thus, the shoulder joint area is stretched and ready for any type of motion the individual might do next during the workout.

For this song, six moves, called the super six, are used to work out all the muscle and joint areas.

- **Straight-leg march**—Students stand straight and gently lift one straight leg out in front, then the other leg. The straight-leg lift stretches out the hip and lower back area. Students reach with the opposite arm to stretch the upper back, shoulders, and arms.

- **Tap behind**—From a standing position, students tap the foot or toe diagonally behind them. This movement stretches out the front of the thigh, hip, knee, and ankle areas. Students should rotate the arms and reach as though they are skating, which stretches out the back and sides (torso or core), shoulders, and arms. (If using a GeoMat, students step on 6 with the right foot, tap the left toe on 9, step to 4 with left foot, and tap 7 with the right toe.)

- **Hand walks**—From a standing position students stretch and place the hands on the floor and walk them forward until students are in a push-up position, then walk them back. They repeat walking them forward and back. This activity works almost all muscles and joint areas. Reaching down stretches out the shoulders and back. Walking forward and backward stretches out the back, neck, shoulders, arms, wrists, hips, legs, and ankles.

- **Torso twists**—From a standing position with the knees bent in a slight squat, students should try to keep the hips and lower body still and twist the upper body or torso from side to side. This stretches out the torso, or core, which is between the shoulders and hips.

- **Arm circles**—In a sitting or standing position, students circle arms forward, then backward slowly and with control. This movement stretches out the shoulders.

- **Heel raises**—Students stand up straight, then lift the heels off the ground, then slowly lower them. They repeat the exercise several times to stretch the ankles and the back of the calves, called the gastrocnemius or gastroc.

This poster is found on the DVD-ROM. It can help students remember possible moves for warming up and dynamically stretching the muscles.

Lyrics and Actions to "Dynamic Stretch"

Lyrics	Actions
Introduction:	
Stretch it	Do diagonal arms (one goes up while the other goes down).
Stretch it, stretch it	With the hands in fists, shake down 4 times. Repeat diagonal arms with the opposite arm going up.
Stretch it	Repeat 4 shakes. Repeat diagonal arms with the opposite arm going up.
Stretch it, stretch it	Repeat 4 shakes.
Chorus:	
Stretch it, stretch it, dynamic stretch	Do diagonal arms (one goes up while the other goes down). With the hands in fists, shake down 4 times.
Prepare your body—there is no catch	Repeat diagonal arms with the opposite arm going up. Repeat 4 shakes.
Stretch it, stretch it—slow and controlled	
But not while your muscles are cold	
Verse 1:	
Straight-leg march—here's how it goes	Alternate lifting the right straight leg in front, then the left straight leg in front.
Opposite arm touches upturned toes	Reach the right hand to the left toe, and the left hand to right toe.
Kick nice and smooth—not too high	
Keep it going—don't be shy	
Repeat first two lines of Chorus.	
Verse 2:	
Tap behind—stretch the front thigh	Start in a narrow stance, bring the right foot back to tap behind the left foot, return to a narrow stance, bring the left foot back to tap behind the right foot, return to a narrow stance. (If using a GeoMat: Step on 5 with the right foot, tap the left toe on 9, step to 5 with the left foot, tap 7 with the right toe.)
It's so easy—give it a try	
Move your arms like you are skating	Alternate moving the arms with one reaching in front and the other reaching back in opposition to the supporting leg.
Slow and controlled—there's no debating	
Repeat first two lines of Chorus.	
Verse 3:	
Hand walks—hands flat on the floor	Stand with the feet together.
Hands walk forward—it's not a chore	Reach over to touch the floor directly in front of the feet, then walk the hands out to a push-up position.
Hands walk back—to your first position	Walk the hands back.

Lyrics	Actions
Do a few more—that's your mission	
Repeat first two lines of Chorus.	Perform another hand walk.
Verse 4:	
Now try the torso twist	Stand with the legs narrow and knees slightly bent; keep the hips stationary so that only the upper body is rotating.
Go slow—I insist	Slowly rotate to one side and look behind.
Look behind for a view	Repeat to the other side.
Now other side—thank you	
Repeat first two lines of Chorus.	
Verse 5:	
Arm circles—standing tall	Circle the arms forward (small).
Circle forward—controlled and small	
Try backward—continue to roll	Circle the arms backward (small).
Shoulders working—still with control	
Repeat first two lines of Chorus.	
Verse 6:	
Heel raises—move up and down	Stand with the feet together. Come up on the toes and elevate the heels off the floor.
Work the gastroc—from the air to the ground	As the heels come off the floor, raise the hands in a biceps curl. As the heels return to the floor, lower the hands.
Up on your toes—it works the calf	
Extend like a giraffe	
Verse 7:	
Now you are prepared to work out	Continue heel raises. As the heels come off the floor, stretch arms over the head. As heels return to the floor, lower the arms.
Be sure to plan your route	Continue heel raises. As the heels come off the floor, raise the hands in a biceps curl. As the heels return to the floor, lower the hands.
Move to the next stage	
Enjoy activities for your age	
Ending:	
Stretch it, stretch it, dynamic stretch	Do diagonal arms (one goes up while the other goes down). With the hands in fists, shake down 4 times.
Stretch it, stretch it, dynamic stretch	Repeat diagonal arms with the opposite arm going up. Repeat 4 shakes.
Stretch it, stretch it	Repeat diagonal arms with the opposite arm going up, with 4 shakes.
Stretch it, stretch it	Repeat diagonal arms with the opposite arm going up, with 4 shakes.

Dynamic Stretch

Assessment 1

Name _____

Draw or describe the joint areas that get stretched by performing the super six exercises.

Straight-leg march	Tap behind	Hand walks
Torso twist	**Arm circles**	**Heel raises**

From GeoMotion Group, Inc., 2012, *Learning through movement and music: Exercise your smarts* (Champaign, IL: Human Kinetics).

Dynamic Stretch

Assessment 2

me _____

1. What do you need to do before a dynamic stretch?
   _____

2. What is the purpose of the dynamic stretch?
   _____

3. How many minutes should you take for the dynamic stretch?
   _____

4. What is the name of the area where two bones come together and are attached by connective tissue?
   _____

5. What are some names of main areas of the body where two or more bones come together and need to be stretched?
   _____

6. Why should you move the body slowly and in control for the dynamic stretch?
   _____

7. Why do you need to move the joint in a full range of motion?
   _____

8. Name the super six exercises.
   1. _____
   2. _____
   3. _____
   4. _____
   5. _____
   6. _____

9. Which of the super six do you think works the most joint areas? Which joint areas can you name?
   _____

From GeoMotion Group, Inc., 2012, *Learning through movement and music: Exercise your smarts* (Champaign, IL: Human Kinetics).

Dynamic Stretch handouts and an answer key for Dynamic Stress Assessment 2 are available on the DVD-ROM. Refer to the Warm-Up and Dynamic Stretch Poster for answers to Dynamic Stretch Assessment 1.

WHERE ARE MY MUSCLES?

n this activity, the muscles and their locations are reviewed. Remember, for an individual to stay in shape, they need to work each muscle or muscle group (see the figures on the Where Are My Muscles poster). Table 4.1 lists the major muscles within each area of the body.

TABLE 4.1
Locations of Muscles

	Upper body	Midsection or core	Lower body
Front of body	• Pectoralis major—upper chest • Biceps—front of upper arm • Deltoid—shoulder	• Rectus abdominis—muscles over the stomach area or the abdominal muscles • Obliques—on each side of the abdominal muscles	Quadriceps—front of the thigh
Back of body	• Triceps—back of upper arm • Latissimus dorsi—along the sides of the upper back • Trapezius—spans the neck, shoulders, and upper back	Erector spinae—along the spine	• Hamstrings—back of the thigh • Gluteus maximus—largest muscle in the buttocks • Gastrocnemius—back of the calf

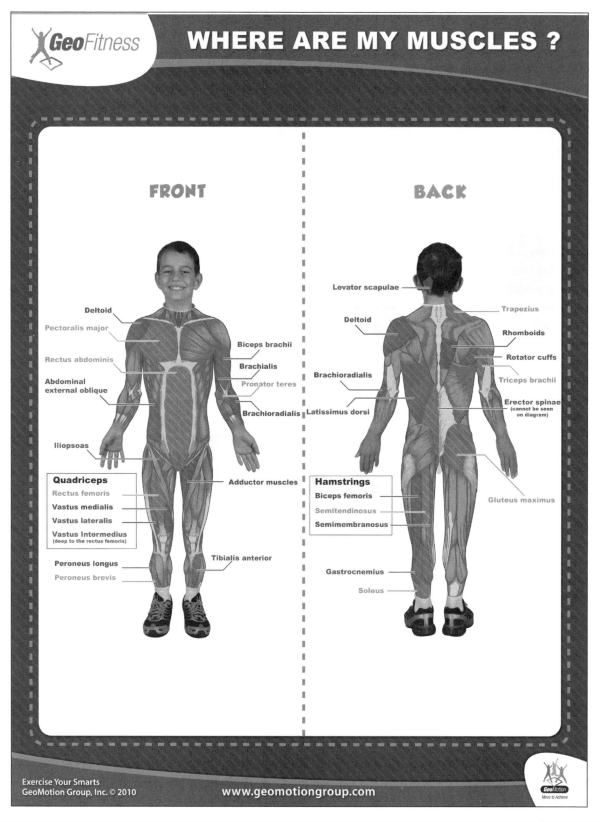

This poster is found on the DVD-ROM. It can be used as a visual to help teach students where their muscles are located.

Lyrics and Actions to "Where Are My Muscles?"

Lyrics	Actions
Chorus:	
Where are my muscles? I'd like to know	Start with the hands out in a questioning position. Gesture down body to feet. Point to the head.
Got some on top and some down below	Point to the upper body; flex the biceps to "make a muscle." Then point to the lower body.
To stay in shape I've got to work them all	Show your muscles (flex the biceps). Point from head to toe.
Tap the muscles as each one I call	Show your muscles (flex the biceps) and put the hands on the hips.
Verse 1:	
Quadriceps are at the front of your thigh	Tap the front upper part of the leg.
Hamstrings are found at the back	Tap the back upper part of the leg.
Gluteus maximus are the muscles in your rear	Tap the rear.
Gastrocnemius is the back of your calf	Tap the back of the calf.
Latissimus dorsi along the sides of the back	Tap the sides of the back.
Erector spinae located along the spine	Tap the spine.
Rectus abdominis is over your stomach	Tap the stomach.
Obliques go down your sides like a line	Slide the hands from the side of the torso to the middle over the stomach.
Pectoralis major is in the chest	Tap the chest.
Trapezius spans the neck, shoulders, and upper back	Tap the upper back.
Biceps and triceps are in your upper arm	Tap the top of the upper arm, then the bottom of the upper arm.
The deltoid is a prime mover for tension or slack	Tap the shoulders.
Chorus:	
Where are my muscles? I'd like to know	Hold the hands out in a questioning position. Point to the head.
Got some on top and some down below	Point to the upper body. Show your muscles (flex the biceps). Then point to the lower body.
To stay in shape I've got to work them all	Show your muscles (flex the biceps). Point from head to toe.
Tap the muscles as each one I call	Show your muscles (flex the biceps) and put the hands on the hips.
Verse 2:	
Quadriceps, gluteus maximus, hamstrings, gastrocnemius, latissimus dorsi, erector spinae Rectus abdominis, obliques, pectoralis major, trapezius, biceps and triceps, deltoid	Point to each muscle as it is reviewed.

Where Are My Muscles?

Assessment

Name _____

Match each muscle with its location.

Muscle	Draw line to show match	Location
1. Quadriceps		a. Back of upper arm
2. Hamstrings		b. Muscles in the rear or buttocks
3. Gluteus maximus		c. Shoulder
4. Gastrocnemius		d. Muscle area over your stomach
5. Latissimus dorsi		e. Back of the thigh
6. Erector spinae		f. Front of the thigh
7. Rectus abdominis		g. Front of upper arm
8. Obliques		h. Back of the calf
9. Pectoralis major		i. On each side of the abdominal muscles
10. Trapezius		j. Upper chest
11. Biceps		k. Spans the neck, shoulders, and upper back
12. Triceps		l. Along the sides of the upper back
13. Deltoid		m. Along the spine

From GeoMotion Group, Inc., 2012, *Learning through movement and music: Exercise your smarts* (Champaign, IL: Human Kinetics).

The Where Are My Muscles? handout and answer key are available on the DVD-ROM.

After a warm-up and a dynamic stretch, an individual is ready for the actual workout. This section provides more information about performing a muscle workout. A person may want to work the skeletal muscles for strength and endurance or perform a cardiovascular workout to improve the heart, lungs, and circulatory system (cardiovascular fitness).

In this activity students work their skeletal muscles. Skeletal muscles are those muscles an individual can feel right under the skin. They are called skeletal muscles because they attach to bones of the skeleton. When a muscle contracts, it shortens and causes the bones at a joint to move.

Skeletal muscles work in pairs to move a bone at a joint area (see figure 5.1 on page 22). One muscle contracts, or shortens, to cause an action at a joint while the opposite muscle relaxes and sometimes lengthens. The contracting muscle is doing the work. One muscle contacts to move part of the body one way, then the opposing muscle contracts to move it back.

What causes the arm to bend and straighten at the elbow? On top of the upper arm is the biceps muscle and on the bottom of the upper arm is the triceps muscle. To move the arm to bend at the elbow, the biceps contracts or shortens while the triceps relaxes. To straighten the arm at the elbow the triceps contracts or shortens while the biceps relaxes.

To exercise a muscle a person must perform repetitions. The term *repetition* (rep) is one completion of an activity or exercise. A rep consists of lifting a weight and returning to the starting position. So, in the case of a push-up where the weight is the individual's own body, the rep would consist of being in the starting push-up position with the arms straight, bending at the elbows to lower the body, then lifting back into the starting position.

When performing an exercise, individuals usually perform more than one rep. A *set* is a group of consecutive repetitions for any exercise. For example, if a person does 10 consecutive push-ups, the person completes 1 set of 10 reps.

A muscle group or body area is the part of the body that is targeted for a specific exercise. Using body regions makes it easier to remember the muscles to ensure a person works all of them. A person should work the chest, shoulders, arms, legs, back (spine), and abdominal muscles. Simply put, the regions to work are the upper body, the midsection (core), and the lower body. Table 5.1 charts the muscles, their locations, and the exercises that can be performed to work them.

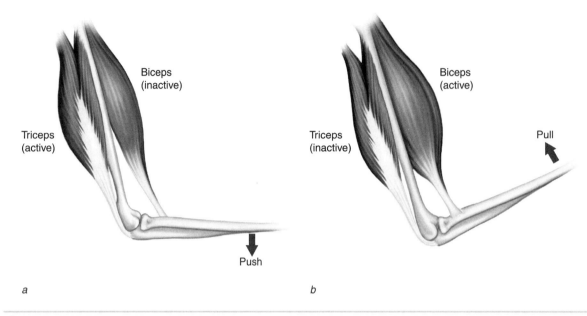

a   *b*

Figure 5.1   Muscles work in pairs to move the bones. In this figure, the biceps and triceps muscles contract (active) or relax (inactive) so that they can bend and straighten the arm.

TABLE 5.1
Muscles and Exercises

Region	Muscle	Location	Action	Exercises
Lower body	Quadriceps (quads)	Thigh Front of upper leg	• Knee extension—straighten, or extend the lower leg • Hip flexion—flex, or bend the hip	• Squat or lunge • Leg press • Leg extension • Going up steps • Jumping
	Gluteus maximus (glutes)	Buttocks Hips (rear)	• Extension of the hip joint—if you are bent over at the hip, it helps you raise your upper body to stand up • If the leg is lifted, glutes contract to bring upper leg back in line	• Lunge or squat • Leg press • Going up steps • Climbing steep incline or hill • Jumping
	Hamstrings	Back of thigh	• Flexes, or bends at the knee joint • Extends, or straightens the hip joint	• Leg curl • Pushing foot on skateboard
	Gastrocnemius	Calf Back of lower leg	• Flexion, or bending at the knee • Plantar flexion (like pressing gas pedal)	• Heel raises • Walking on tiptoes

Region	Muscle	Location	Action	Exercises
Midsection or core	Latissimus dorsi (lats)	Sides of upper back	Helps pull the upper arm at the shoulder joint down or toward the chest	• Rowing canoe or kayak • Pull-up—hands face away from you while gripping the bar • Chin-up—hands face toward you while gripping the bar
	Erector spinae	Back Spine	• Extends, or straightens the vertebral column • Back extension	• Superman • Back hyperextension or lifts
	Rectus abdominis	Over the stomach	Flexion, or bending forward of the trunk	Curl-ups, or crunches
	Obliques	Sides of abdominal area Waist	• Rotates torso • Side flexion, or bending sideways	• Torso twist • Side bend
Upper body	Pectoralis major	Upper chest	• Flexes the humerus at shoulder • Extends the humerus at shoulder • Adducts and medially rotates the humerus at shoulder	• Push-ups • Dips on parallel bars • Chest or bench press
	Trapezius	Upper limbs Upper back	• Retraction of scapula or bringing shoulder blades toward each other • Helps pull toward the body from above	• Shoulder shrugs • Upright rows
	Deltoid	Shoulder	Moves arm away from the body at the shoulder	• Lateral arm raises • Front arm raises • Shoulder press
	Biceps	Upper arm	• Flexes, or bends elbow • Assists in raising arm at the shoulder	Arm curl
	Triceps	Upper arm	• Extends, or straightens arm at elbow • Brings arm closer to the body from the shoulder	• Triceps dip • Triceps extension • Triceps push-down

Lyrics	Actions
Verse 1:	
Know your muscles—how to keep them strong	Begin marching.
Exercise correctly and you can't go wrong	Continue marching and show your muscles (flex the biceps).
Skeletal muscle—you can see and feel	Show your muscles (flex the biceps) on one arm.
Bodybuilders look like they're made of steel	Bring up the other arm and show your muscles (flex the biceps). Bring the elbows in together, then back out to show the biceps muscle.
Muscle workout—muscle workout—muscle workout	Show your muscles (flex the biceps) on one arm. Bring up the other arm and show your muscles (flex the biceps). Bring the elbows in together 2 times.
Strong muscles with a muscle workout	Show your muscles (flex the biceps) on one arm. Bring up the other arm and show your muscles (flex the biceps). Bring the elbows in together 2 times.
Verse 2:	
The term *repetition's* also called a rep	Do toe taps. (If using a GeoMat, do toe taps on 2.)
One completion or just one step	
10 to 12 reps is called a set	Do overhead presses with alternating knee lifts.
Many sets will work up a sweat	
Verse 3:	
Muscles give us motion—work by contracting	Do alternating side touches with lateral arm raises.
Shorten to do work—that's how they're acting	
Work in pairs—one moves one way	Get into a small lunge position and imitate dumbbell rows.
Opposite contracts—moves it back, they say	
Verse 4:	
Many muscle regions to work	Switch sides to imitate the row with the other arm.
Leg, back, abdominals—do not shirk	
Chest, shoulders, and arms, too	
Let's work each region—that's what we'll do	Stand with the feet together and imitate chest presses.
Verse 5:	
The first region is your lower body	Hold up 1 finger, then point to the lower body.
The second is your midsection or core	Hold up 2 fingers, then point to the midsection.
The third is your upper parts	Hold up 3 fingers, then point to upper body and show your muscles (flex the biceps).
There are 3 regions and no more	
Verse 6:	
Quadriceps are called a quad	Point to the front of the upper thigh.
The front of the thigh and it's a little odd	Perform small squats.

Lyrics	Actions
Really four muscles I confess	
Squats work here or a leg press	
Verse 7:	
Gluteus maximus—big muscles in your rear	Point to the buttocks or rear.
Called the glutes but have no fear	Perform a small lunge with biceps curls; make sure the front knee does not go past 90 degrees and that the knee does not go past the toe.
Make them stronger with a squat or lunge	
These are big muscles, so take the plunge	
Verse 8:	
Hamstrings are back of your thighs	Point to the back of the upper thigh. Alternate standing leg curls with biceps curls.
These three muscles are quite some size	
They straighten the hip or bend the knee	
Do a leg curl we all agree	
Verse 9:	
Gastrocnemius is the back of your calf	Point to the back of the lower leg (calf).
From knee to heel, one leg makes half	Perform heel raises up and down.
Heel raises make gastrocs have great shape	
If you need to run fast you can escape	
Verse 10:	
Latissimus dorsi—sides of the back	Point to the lats along the sides of the back.
This muscle is also known as lats	Bend forward with one hand used for support on the thigh and the other imitating a dumbbell row.
A good exercise is dumbbell rows	
One side for 10 then switch—I suppose	Switch arms and perform dumbbell rows.
Verse 11:	
Erector spinae—located along the spine	
Keep these muscles strong and things will be fine	Point to the muscles along the spine.
Lie on your stomach—lift your legs is the plan	Lie on the stomach and lift the legs.
Slowly lift arms, too—look like Superman	Lift the arms so that both the legs and arms are off floor.
Verse 12:	
Work your rectus abdominis—they are long and flat	Turn over and lay on the back with the knees bent and the feet on the floor in a curl-up position.
Try curl-ups or sit-ups while on a mat	Have the hands out parallel to the legs and lift up the upper back and shoulder region to move the hands forward about 3 inches (7.62 cm).
Abdominal workouts help strengthen your core	Repeat the curl-up.

(continued)

Lyrics	Actions
You'll feel so strong that you'll want to do more	
Verse 13:	
On your sides are obliques	Move into a kneeling position and point to the obliques (front sides of the abdominal region).
If they are fit you can really look chic	Rotate the torso from side to side.
Rotate your torso from side to side	
These strong muscles will be your pride	
Verse 14:	
The pectoralis major is in the chest	Point to the muscles in the chest.
It covers the front like a short vest	
Build this muscle with push-ups or dips	Get into a regular or modified push-up position. Perform push-ups.
Listen to your coach to get the latest tips	
Verse 15:	
Trapezius spans the neck, shoulders, upper back	Stand up and point to the upper back area.
Moves shoulder blades toward the spine—that's a fact	
Perform shoulder shrugs or upright rows	Perform upright rows.
Try the exercise, many reps of those	
Verse 16:	
The deltoid a prime mover to lift your arm	Point to the shoulder area.
Helps lift bales down on the farm	Perform overhead presses.
Lateral raises are called the shoulder fly	
See how it works when you lift toward the sky	Perform lateral raises by bringing both arms up, parallel to ground.
Verse 17:	
Biceps and triceps are in your upper arm	Perform alternating biceps curls.
They work in opposition just like a charm	
Biceps on top and triceps below	Point to the biceps, then triceps.
They work together to help you throw	Perform alternating biceps curls.
Verse 18:	
Review these muscles—point to each part	Touch each muscle in the review.
If you need to, look at a chart	
Quadriceps, gluteus maximus, hamstrings,	
gastrocnemius, latissimus dorsi, erector spinae,	
rectus abdominis, obliques, pectoralis, trapezius,	
deltoid, biceps and triceps	
Muscle, muscle, muscle workout!	Show the biceps muscles.

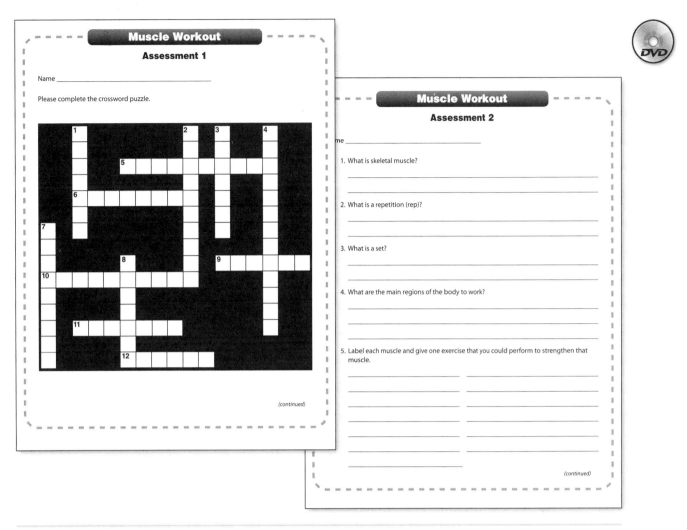

Muscle Workout

Assessment 1

Name _____

Please complete the crossword puzzle.

(continued)

Muscle Workout

Assessment 2

Name _____

1. What is skeletal muscle?

_____

_____

2. What is a repetition (rep)?

_____

_____

3. What is a set?

_____

_____

4. What are the main regions of the body to work?

_____

_____

_____

5. Label each muscle and give one exercise that you could perform to strengthen that muscle.

_____   _____

_____   _____

_____   _____

_____   _____

_____   _____

_____

(continued)

Muscle Workout handouts and answer keys are available on the DVD-ROM.

ACTIVITY

6

CARDIO MARCH

Dr. John Ratey is an associate clinical professor of psychiatry at Harvard Medical School. He has authored many books related to the importance of physical activity and the brain. His publications explain how exercise is crucial for the brain and body to work at peak performance. He says that there is a "connection between exercise and the brain's performance that shows how even moderate exercise will supercharge mental circuits to beat stress, sharpen thinking, enhance memory, and much more" (2008).

After a warm-up and a dynamic stretch a person is ready for the actual workout. A person may want to work the muscles for strength and endurance or perform a cardiovascular workout to improve cardiovascular fitness (heart, lungs, and circulatory system).

Cardiovascular fitness is thought to be the most important component of physical fitness. It is considered the best indicator of overall health. Cardiovascular fitness is often called cardiorespiratory or aerobic fitness.

Cardio refers to the heart and *vascular* refers to the blood and circulatory system. The heart is a muscle (cardiac muscle), and just like a person's skeletal muscles, it gets stronger when it is worked. When performing a cardiovascular workout, a person is exercising the heart and circulating the blood.

Aerobic exercises are best for developing cardiovascular fitness. *Aerobic* means "with oxygen" and includes continuous activities that use oxygen. That means that breathing may become more difficult, but a person should still able to talk while exercising. If it gets to the point where a person is exercising too hard to talk, then the exercise has become anaerobic. Aerobic exercise (with oxygen) can reduce the risk of death due to cardiovascular problems in the following ways:

- strengthens the heart,
- improves circulation,
- reduces blood pressure,
- facilitates the transport of oxygen to all parts of the body,
- facilitates flow of air in and out of the lungs,

- reduces the risk of diabetes,
- reduces stress,
- improves the ability for muscles to use fat as energy during exercise,
- improves aerobic capacity, and
- lowers the incidence of depression.

Anaerobic exercise is exercise without enough oxygen circulating through the body; the body can keep that pace for only a short time. This means that even if students are doing an activity that is typically considered a part of a cardiovascular workout (such as running), but are doing it at extreme levels of intensity (like sprinting), the activity is actually *not* a part of a cardiovascular workout. For example, when running as fast as possible, eventually a person reaches a point where keeping up the pace is impossible; without enough oxygen, the body slows down. Usually athletes perform anaerobic drills since sprinting types of activities are needed in sporting events.

Every person should try to exercise 60 minutes a day. For a cardiovascular workout, individuals should perform most of the exercise at a rate that is called *moderate to vigorous*. *Moderate* means breathing at a somewhat fast pace (6-7 on a perceived exertion scale) (see the Perceived Exertion Method poster on the DVD-ROM). *Vigorous* means an even faster pace but not so fast that talking is impossible while still exercising (8-9 on a perceived exertion scale).

Cardiovascular exercise improves aerobic capacity. Aerobic capacity is how well the heart, lungs, and blood vessels work together and is defined as the maximum amount of oxygen the body can use during a specified period. Typically, the more fit an individual is, the higher that individual's aerobic capacity.

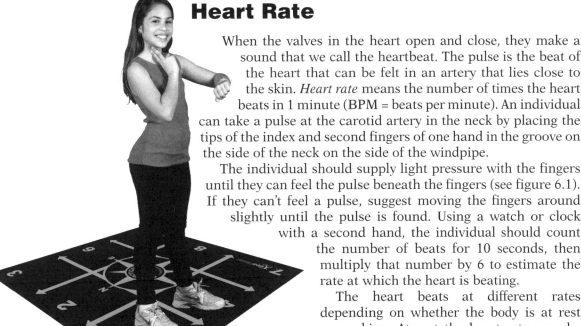

Heart Rate

When the valves in the heart open and close, they make a sound that we call the heartbeat. The pulse is the beat of the heart that can be felt in an artery that lies close to the skin. *Heart rate* means the number of times the heart beats in 1 minute (BPM = beats per minute). An individual can take a pulse at the carotid artery in the neck by placing the tips of the index and second fingers of one hand in the groove on the side of the neck on the side of the windpipe.

The individual should supply light pressure with the fingers until they can feel the pulse beneath the fingers (see figure 6.1). If they can't feel a pulse, suggest moving the fingers around slightly until the pulse is found. Using a watch or clock with a second hand, the individual should count the number of beats for 10 seconds, then multiply that number by 6 to estimate the rate at which the heart is beating.

The heart beats at different rates depending on whether the body is at rest or working. At rest the heart rate may be beating from around 70 to 85 BPM (or for 11 to 14 beats/10 sec). As an individual exercises, the heart rate increases.

Figure 6.1 Taking the pulse at the carotid artery.

Courtesy of GeoMotion Group, Inc. Available: http://www.GeoMotiongroup.com/product/exercise-your-smarts-8-pack-poster

Target Heart Rate

The heart circulates blood throughout the entire body, so the heart adjusts and speeds up or slows down depending on how hard an individual is working. A person's heart rate constantly changes while exercising, depending on whether the exercise is light, moderate, or vigorous. As soon as a person stops working to rest or take a break, the heart begins to slow down. So, if a person wants to measure the exercising heart rate, it must be done immediately upon stopping work; the person counts for 10 seconds (then multiplies by 6) to estimate how many BPM the heart was beating during work.

Monitoring the heart rate is one way to determine the intensity or how hard a person is working. To get the best cardiovascular workout that has health benefits, an individual should work in a target heart rate zone. It is recommended that individuals work at 60 to 85% of their maximum heart rate, or HRmax. To determine the different percentages, a mathematical calculation is required. To make it easier, charts such as table 6.1 have been developed to show what a person's heart rate should be for ages 10 to 25.

For an 8- to 12-year-old the target heart rate zone would be approximately 125 to 180 BPM. In other words, when taking the pulse, the person would count 21 to 30 heartbeats in 10 seconds. If a person is at a rate above or below the target, exercise must be adjusted. At the target heart rate, the heart works twice as hard as when the body is at rest. This type of cardiovascular workout makes the heart stronger.

Perceived Exertion Method

Another way to calculate how hard a person is working is to use a perceived exertion scale (see the Perceived Exertion Method poster). This kind of scale asks a person to think about the question, "On a scale of 1 to 10, how hard do you feel you are working?" The individual determines the perceived level of exertion. This method is based on how fast a person is breathing, how fast the heart is beating, and how intense the work feels. When using a perceived exertion scale, students should work at 6 or 7 for a moderate and 8 or 9 for a vigorous cardiovascular workout.

An individual can use a scale of 1 to 10; 10 is the hardest. If a person perceives not working hard at all, the person might be at a 1 or 2. If the intensity gets a bit higher, the person might perceive a 3 or 4. If the person perceives working hard but is still able to talk while performing the exercise (called the *talk test*), the person would be below a 9. If the person cannot talk, then the person is at a 9 or 10.

TABLE 6.1
Target Heart Rate

Age	Target heart rate zone 60%–85%	10-second count
10	126–178 BPM	21–30
15	123–174 BPM	20–29
20	120–170 BPM	20–28
25	117–166 BPM	19–28

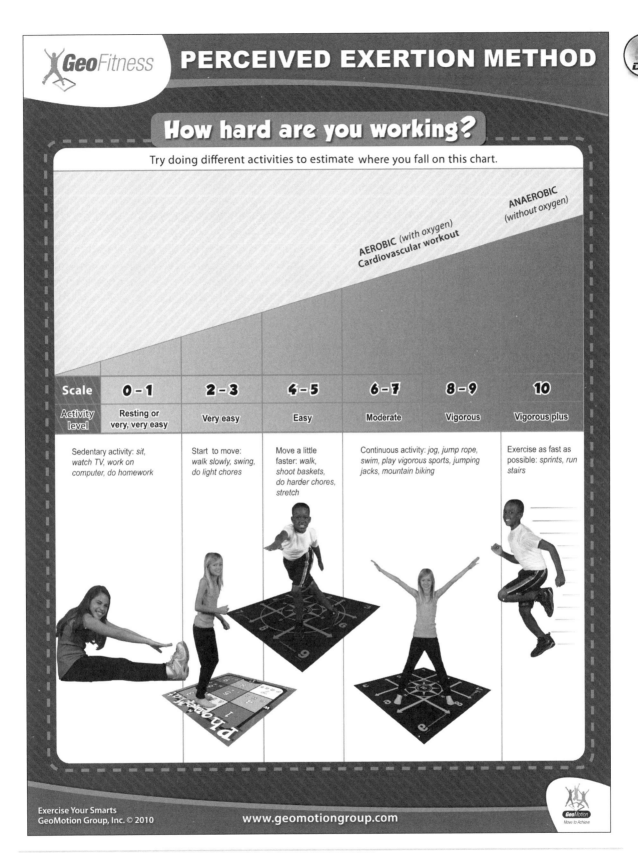

PERCEIVED EXERTION METHOD

How hard are you working?

Try doing different activities to estimate where you fall on this chart.

AEROBIC (with oxygen)
Cardiovascular workout

ANAEROBIC (without oxygen)

Scale	0 – 1	2 – 3	4 – 5	6 – 7	8 – 9	10
Activity level	Resting or very, very easy	Very easy	Easy	Moderate	Vigorous	Vigorous plus

Sedentary activity: *sit, watch TV, work on computer, do homework*

Start to move: *walk slowly, swing, do light chores*

Move a little faster: *walk, shoot baskets, do harder chores, stretch*

Continuous activity: *jog, jump rope, swim, play vigorous sports, jumping jacks, mountain biking*

Exercise as fast as possible: *sprints, run stairs*

Exercise Your Smarts
GeoMotion Group, Inc. © 2010
www.geomotiongroup.com

GeoMotion
Move to Achieve

This poster is found on the DVD-ROM and can help students learn how to use the perceived exertion method during cardiovascular activity.

Lyrics and Actions to "Cardio March"

Lyrics	Actions
Verse 1:	
You need to exercise 60 minutes a day	March in place; do a narrow march until the chorus. (If using a GeoMat, march on 5.)
Fitness activities, games, or play	
Aerobics should make up most of the hour	
Moderate to vigorous will empower	
Chorus:	
Cardio, cardio, cardio march	Perform X step 2 times with a left-foot lead. 1 rep = forward wide march, step back narrow march, step back wide march, step forward narrow march, stepping every 2 beats. (If using a GeoMat, march on 1,3,5,5,7,9,5,5.)
Move, move, pump your heart	
March, march, cardio march	
Cardio, cardio, cardio march	
Verse 2:	
Cardiovascular is often used	Step forward with one foot and then step back onto the other foot (if using a GeoMat, use 2 and 5). Step forward with the opposite foot and back onto the other foot every 4 counts.
Means the same as aerobics, so don't be confused	
Cardio for short—which refers to the heart	
If you understand this—it makes you smart	
Repeat Chorus.	Perform X step 2 times with a right-foot lead. 1 rep = forward wide march, step back narrow march, step back wide march, step forward narrow march, stepping every 2 beats. (If using a GeoMat, march on 3,1,5,5,9,7,5,5.)
Verse 3:	
Your cardiovascular system delivers oxygen	Narrow march for four beats, step right and narrow march for four more beats, and step right and narrow march for four more beats. Then jump back to the left. (If using a GeoMat, march on 4, 5, 6 and jump back to 4). Do 3 times and repeat through verse 4.
To the muscles so work can be done	
The most important thing for an aerobic activity	
Is continuously moving—that's the key	
Verse 4:	
When you do physical activity—your heart rate quickens	

Lyrics	Actions
Breathing gets deeper—using the cardiovascular system	
Staying aerobic—means with oxygen	
You'll be able to tell—you can do it with a grin	March on 5.
Repeat Chorus.	Perform X step 2 times with a left-foot lead. 1 rep = forward wide march, step back narrow march, step back wide march, step forward narrow march, stepping every 2 beats. (If using a GeoMat, march on 1,3,5,5,7,9,5,5.)
Verse 5:	
If you are aerobic—you can pass the talk test	Narrow march for four beats, step left and narrow march for four more beats, and step left and narrow march for four more beats. Then jump back to the right. (If using a GeoMat, march on 6, 5, 4 and jump back to 4.) Do 3 times and repeat through verse 6.
Talk while moving without too much stress	
If you're exercising at a rate where you're breathless	
Then you're pushing too hard—ease up I suggest	
Verse 6:	
On a scale of 1 to 10—try for 7 or 8	
You'll see that it is the most effective rate	
You can also stay in your target heart rate zone	March around in a circle.
It's the best method today that is known	
Verse 7:	
Target heart rate is the range of heartbeats	Change direction and march the other direction in a circle.
Heart rate continues and repeats	
60 to 85 percent of your heart rate max	Change direction and march the other direction in a circle.
Use that rate—don't relax	
Verse 8:	
To know your heart rate—you need to know	March in a circle with knee lifts.
How to take the pulse of your blood flow	
How many beats is your heart beating?	March in a circle with straight legs.
How much work are you achieving?	
Extra Bridge of Music	Jog in a circle.
Verse 9:	
One location for a pulse check	Jog in a circle in the other direction.
Is the carotid artery on the side of your neck	
Place two fingers gently to feel	March in place.

(continued)

Lyrics	Actions
Count the beats—that's the deal	March in a square, 4 beats for each location. (If using GeoMat, march on 1, march on 3, march on 9, march on 7.)
Verse 10:	
Count for 10 seconds, then multiply by 6	
That equals the times per minute your heart ticks	
Use this number to be your guide	Change direction for the square step.
How to exercise your heart is for you to decide	
Verse 11:	
Continuous activity is your goal	
Remember, you are the one in control	
Try speed walking, jogging, riding your bike,	Change direction for the square step.
Jump rope, swimming, dancing, and things you like	
Verse 12:	
So many benefits—exercise regularly	
Better fitness and aerobic capacity	March in place. (If using a GeoMat, march on 5.)
Lower blood pressure—one of the things it will do	March with the knees high.
It will reduce your risk of heart attack, too	
Verse 13:	
Increased bone mass means strong bones, you see	Pretend to jump rope.
You may also live longer—significantly	Pretend to swim.
May help to control your weight	Pretend to jump on a pogo stick.
Just be careful of what you put on your plate	Do slow jumping jacks.
Verse 14:	
Improved thinking, learning, and memory	
Say the experts—like Dr. Ratey	
Release of endorphins by the pituitary gland	Pretend to bicycle.
Makes you happy—makes you feel grand	
Verse 15:	
So exercising makes you feel great	Jog in place.
Your mood enhanced—so don't wait	
Try to exercise most every day	March with high knees.
Mix it up—have fun—do it your way!!	
Ending:	
Cardio, cardio, march, march	
Move, move, pump your heart	Show pumping heart while still marching.
Cardio march	Show biceps muscles.

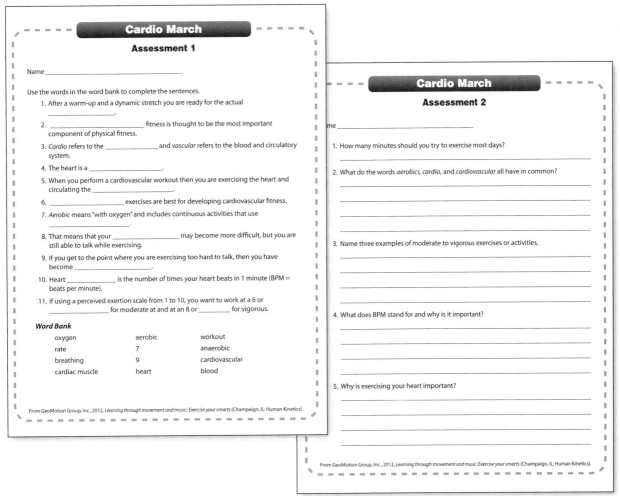

Cardio March

Assessment 1

Name _____

Use the words in the word bank to complete the sentences.

1. After a warm-up and a dynamic stretch you are ready for the actual
_____.

2. _____ fitness is thought to be the most important
component of physical fitness.

3. *Cardio* refers to the _____ and *vascular* refers to the blood and circulatory
system.

4. The heart is a _____.

5. When you perform a cardiovascular workout then you are exercising the heart and
circulating the _____.

6. _____ exercises are best for developing cardiovascular fitness.

7. *Aerobic* means "with oxygen" and includes continuous activities that use
_____.

8. That means that your _____ may become more difficult, but you are
still able to talk while exercising.

9. If you get to the point where you are exercising too hard to talk, then you have
become _____.

10. Heart _____ is the number of times your heart beats in 1 minute (BPM =
beats per minute).

11. If using a perceived exertion scale from 1 to 10, you want to work at a 6 or
_____ for moderate at and at an 8 or _____ for vigorous.

Word Bank

oxygen	aerobic	workout
rate	7	anaerobic
breathing	9	cardiovascular
cardiac muscle	heart	blood

From GeoMotion Group, Inc., 2012, *Learning through movement and music: Exercise your smarts* (Champaign, IL: Human Kinetics).

Cardio March

Assessment 2

_me _____

1. How many minutes should you try to exercise most days?
_____

2. What do the words *aerobics, cardio,* and *cardiovascular* all have in common?
_____
_____
_____
_____

3. Name three examples of moderate to vigorous exercises or activities.
_____
_____
_____
_____

4. What does BPM stand for and why is it important?
_____
_____
_____
_____

5. Why is exercising your heart important?
_____
_____
_____
_____
_____

From GeoMotion Group, Inc., 2012, *Learning through movement and music: Exercise your smarts* (Champaign, IL: Human Kinetics).

Cardio March handouts and answer keys are available on the DVD-ROM.

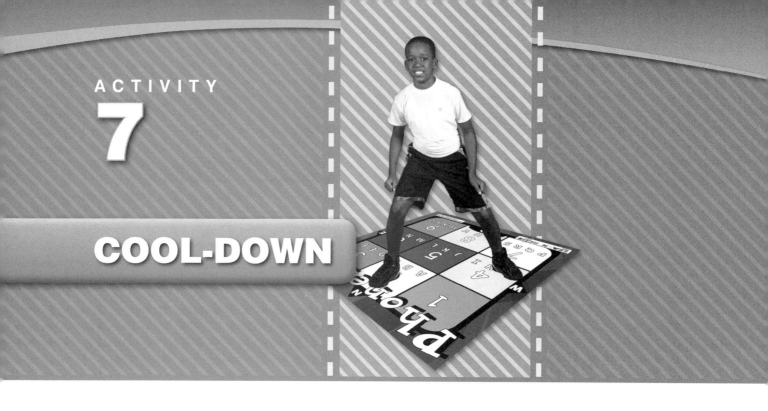

COOL-DOWN

A cool-down is a period of activity that allows the body to slow down and recover from exercise. After a workout, a person needs to gradually slow down with a walk, slow jog, or other type of low-intensity exercise. These exercises and activities are very similar to ones in the warm-up phase prior to exercise.

To achieve the cool-down individuals need to slow down their movement to a low intensity for 3 to 5 minutes. The heart rate should decrease and breathing should return to normal.

Remember, the purpose is to allow the body to slow down, specifically the heart to beat slower. The decrease in blood circulation allows the body to recover. Individuals can usually tell because their breathing will slow down, and their heart will also beat slower. They should not sit down or stop moving until their body has recovered.

The gradual decrease and slower movements at a low intensity will prevent blood from pooling in the legs. Blood pooling happens when an exerciser stops too quickly while the heart rate is still high and pumping large amounts of blood to the heart. The blood collects in the large veins of the legs. If this happens, a person may feel lightheaded because blood is not reaching the heart and brain as effectively.

The reason individuals need to cool down for at least 3 minutes is that it takes the body that long to recover. Once the body has recovered, the muscles are still warm. This is the best time to go to the next phase of the exercise bout to increase flexibility—the static stretch.

Another purpose for a brief cool-down session is during a workout that includes anaerobic activity. Sometimes during a workout students might find themselves working at an intensity level of 10. When they work that hard, after about 20 to 30 seconds they should be breathing so fast that they cannot carry on a conversation and begin to feel breathless. At this point, they will have reached what is called the *anaerobic threshold* (or lactic acid threshold), which means they won't have enough oxygen to keep up the pace. During this time of working anaerobically, lactic acid starts to accumulate in the muscles and the muscles become starved for oxygen. At this time, a short cool-down period is needed to allow the body to slow down and recover. Once it has, the oxygen will be replenished, the lactic acid moved out of the muscles, and students can again try to go at the fast pace.

This poster, found on the DVD-ROM, is a fun visual to use in the classroom to help students remember ways to cool down the body. It also contains examples of static stretches, which can be used after cool-down and in activity 8.

Lyrics and Actions to "Cool-Down"

Lyrics	Actions
Introduction:	
Cool-down	
Cool	Step tap in front.
Chorus:	
It's a cool-down thing—my breathing's getting slower	
I'm recovering—my heart rate's getting lower	Continue step tap with a heart pump action. Take the hands lower and lower.
I am moving slower—at a low intensity	Step tap in front.
Circulating blood—throughout all of me	Hold the palms facing out and make circles while continuing to step tap.
Verse 1:	
After your workout—you need to cool down	Do wide step taps with a hitchhiking motion.
You need to keep moving—can't go to the ground	
Slow down your movements to help you recover	
It helps avoid stiffness—you will discover	
Verse 2:	
Exercise similar to the warm-up but slower	Do alternate knee lifts.
Your heart rate will drop and get lower and lower	Do a heart pump action and take the hands lower and lower.
Try a slow jog—slow down even more	Do a slow jog in place.
Then walk in a circle around the floor	Walk around in a small circle.
Verse 3:	
Reach your arms up high toward the sky	Reach alternating arms high while walking.
Then place them on your head—give it a try	Place the hands on the head while walking.
Inhale and exhale—slow down your breathing	Spread the arms out wide for exhale and bring them together for inhale.
That's the effect you want to be achieving	
Repeat Chorus.	
Verse 4:	
Walking around keeps the blood from pooling	Walk in a circle.
The entire time your body is cooling	
The blood moves waste products—keeps your body clean	
Like lactic acid—so you know what I mean	Change direction.

Lyrics	Actions
Verse 5:	
Step touch side to side—tap your toe	
Swing your arms gently—try several in a row	Step right, tap left toe, step left, tap right toe. (If using a GeoMat, step right on 6, tap left toe on 6, step left on 4, tap right toe on 4.) Swing the arms to the tempo of the step taps.
Now tap your heel—crossing over in front	Take the heels and cross over on the tap. (If using a GeoMat, step right on 6, tap the left heel on 3, step left on 4, tap right heel on 1.)
This may seem like an acrobatic stunt	
Tapping backward and diagonally behind	Take the toe and cross behind on the tap. (If using a GeoMat, step right on 6, tap the left toe on 9, step left on 4, tap the right toe on 7.)
Gives a good stretch—you will find	
Move your arms like you are skating	Add more arm movements.
Slow and controlled—there's no debating	
Repeat Chorus.	
Verse 6:	
Leave your legs out wide—perform a squat	Step out into a wide stance.
Look straight ahead and focus on a spot	Perform squats with the hands on the upper thighs.
When you descend think about sitting in a chair	
Don't let your knees go past your toes—careful—beware	
Verse 7:	
When you straighten your legs, lift your arms chest high	As the legs straighten, lift the arms up to chest height.
Move up and down—you may feel it in your thigh	
Hold the squat position, then shift side to side	Stay in a squat position; shift the squat side to side.
Squat a little more—you decide	
Verse 8:	
When your heart rate slows and you feel more relaxed	
Your breathing is easy—you don't feel so taxed	
Now you are ready to improve your flexibility	March in place.
A static stretch will help you later with your fitness ability	
Repeat Chorus.	

Cool-Down

Assessment 1

Name _____

TRUE OR FALSE

Circle the correct answer.

T F 1. The goal of the cool-down is to allow the body to speed up and prepare for exercise.

T F 2. The exercises and activities for the cool-down are very similar to the exercises and activities for the warm-up phase before exercise.

T F 3. To cool down you slow your movement to a low intensity for 30 to 45 minutes.

T F 4. During the cool-down, your heart rate should get higher and your breathing should get faster.

T F 5. The purpose of the cool-down is to allow the body to slow down, specifically the heart to beat slower.

T F 6. Do not sit down or stop moving until the body has cooled down and recovered.

T F 7. The gradual decrease and slower movements at a low intensity will prevent blood from pooling in the legs.

T F 8. Blood pooling happens when you stop too quickly and your heart rate is still high and pumping large amounts of blood to the heart.

T F 9. The reason that you need to cool down for at least 3 minutes is that it takes the body that long to recover.

T F 10. The cool-down is the last part of the exercise bout.

Cool-Down

Assessment 2

Name _____

1. What is the goal of the cool-down?

_____

_____

_____

2. How long should the cool-down last? Why?

_____

_____

_____

3. The cool-down should be at a low intensity. Why?

_____

_____

_____

4. What are some types of exercise you might perform for a cool-down?

_____

_____

_____

5. What happens to your heart rate and breathing during the cool-down?

_____

_____

6. What comes after the cool-down?

_____

Cool-Down handouts and answer keys are available on the DVD-ROM.

STATIC STRETCH

Once a person has cooled down and the body has recovered, the static stretching phase should begin. The goal of the static stretch is to improve flexibility. To reach this goal, the person should stretch at each major joint of the body and hold the stretch to allow time for the muscle to lengthen and relax. Each stretch should be held for at least 10 seconds and up to 60 seconds.

The static stretch is an extension, or next step, of the cool-down. The cool-down is performed first to allow the heart to slow down the circulation of blood to the body and allow the body to recover. Once the heart rate is at the preexercise level the static stretch is then performed for an additional 3 to 5 minutes.

Performing a static stretch may help reduce stiffness or muscle soreness. It is also the best time to work on becoming flexible because the muscles are still warm after a workout and cool-down.

Static stretching involves stretching slowly, smoothly, and in a sustained manner to the farthest point, then holding the position for 10 to 60 seconds. For the best results, a person should rest a few seconds, then repeat the stretch. As the muscle relaxes, the person can try to stretch a little farther.

A person should never force a stretch or continue stretching when feeling pain. The goal of stretching is to lengthen the muscle. If a person feels pain, a reflex (called the *stretch reflex*) causes the muscle to contract, or shorten. At that point, the individual is contracting the muscles instead of relaxing, lengthening, and increasing flexibility.

Many injuries related to improper stretching are cumulative and can cause degenerative effects over time. Since there are many safe exercises and exercises that can be made safe with just a few alterations, it is best to ensure the safety of all by avoiding contraindicated exercises. See table 8.1 on page 42 for a few stretches and exercises to avoid.

TABLE 8.1
Contraindicated Exercises and Stretches

Avoid	Try this instead
Neck rolls	To protect the cervical spine from injury, only perform neck movements that look over the shoulder, to the front, and over the other shoulder or that bring ear to shoulder.
Standing toe touches	It is safer to perform toe touches from a sitting or lying position; standing, unsupported toe touches may cause additional stress to the back due to "hanging" on 2 or 3 vertebrae.
Standing windmills	To avoid stress to the back, it is better to perform sitting windmills using slow, controlled movements.
Waist circles and back bends	Arching at the neck or lower back provides strain to the vertebrae; waist circles and back bends are not recommended.
Deep knee bends or lunges	To avoid too much stress on the knee joint, keep the knees behind the toes.
Hurdler stretch	To avoid too much torque on the knee, bend and tuck the leg in front instead of behind.
Double-leg lifts	To avoid arching or overstressing the back, bend one leg and engage the abdominals.

COOL-DOWN AND STATIC STRETCH

DVD

COOL-DOWN — HELPS BODY RECOVER FROM THE WORKOUT

★ **Purpose:** *Low-intensity exercise (similar to warm-up) removes exercise waste products and allows heart rate, circulation, and breathing to slow down.*

★ Jogging | ★ Walking | ★ Step touch | ★ Tap behind | ★ Squats

STATIC STRETCH — IMPROVES FLEXIBILITY

★ **Purpose:** *Stretches for each muscle and joint area to lengthen working muscles and improve flexibility. Make sure heart rate is at preexercise level.*

SITTING TOE TOUCHES | SITTING STRADDLE TOE TOUCHES | QUAD STRETCH | SHOULDER AND UPPER BACK STRETCH

GOOD MORNING STRETCH | TRICEPS STRETCH | REACH ACROSS STRETCH | CHEST STRETCH

NECK STRETCH CHIN OVER SHOULDER | | BUTTERFLY STRETCH |

Exercise Your Smarts
GeoMotion Group, Inc. © 2010

www.geomotiongroup.com

GeoMotion
Move to Achieve

You can use the Cool-Down and Static Stretch poster to help students remember different static stretches that they can perform once they have cooled down their bodies from exercise. It also contains examples of ways they can cool down, which can be used with activity 7.

Lyrics and Actions to "Static Stretch"

Lyrics	Actions
Introduction:	
Static stretch	Stretch the arms overhead.
Verse 1:	
After you cool down, your muscles are still warm	Reach one arm up.
Receptive to stretching—so use good form	Switch sides.
During your workout muscles shorten and contract	Do a chest stretch by clasping the hands behind the back and lifting them up and away from the body.
If you don't stretch them, you'll leave them like that	Reach one arm up.
Verse 2:	
Hold each stretch 10 seconds or more	Reach the other arm up.
You should not feel pain—I implore	Reach both arms up.
If it hurts, back off till you feel only tension	Reach one arm up, then reach the other arm up.
Hope this news gets your attention	Do a chest stretch by placing your hands behind your waist and gently arching your back.
Verse 3:	
Toe touches are safer when you sit	Do sitting toe touches.
Extend your arms as far as your back will permit	
For this hamstring stretch, slightly bend at the knee	
Keep toes flexed to stretch calves, I decree	
Verse 4:	
Put your legs in straddle—legs are wide	Do straddle toe touches to one side.
Reach and rotate hand to one side	
Reach for your toes—as far as you can bend	
Keep knees soft—don't hyperextend	
Verse 5:	
Now rotate to the other leg	Stretch to the other side.
C'mon do it—I don't want to beg	
You should feel your muscles more relaxed	
You can feel it especially in your back	
Verse 6:	
Try the quad stretch—lying down or from a stand	Lie on one side and do a quad stretch with the top leg while using the bottom leg for balance and stability.
Grab one ankle with the alternate hand	
Bend at the knees—bring your foot toward your rear	
Relaxing the muscles—be gentle, you hear	

Lyrics	Actions
Verse 7:	
Use your other hand—stretch the opposite thigh	Switch to the other leg.
Stretching this muscle will help you stay spry	
Keep your knees together side by side	
This stretch is much better, it can't be denied	
Verse 8:	
Shoulders and upper back stretches next, I say	Stretch the back.
Invert the hands in front and gently press away	
You should feel it mainly in your upper back	
That tells you, you are on the right track	
Verse 9:	
Try the good morning stretch—stretch up high	Stretch overhead.
Higher and higher—up toward the sky	
Press from the shoulders and really extend	
Arms are straight—do not bend	
Verse 10:	
Pretend to have an itch between your shoulder blades	Do a triceps stretch on one side.
Bring one hand down—use your other as an aide	
Reach for that spot as far as you can go	
Lengthen your triceps like a stretched bow	
Verse 11:	
Now switch hands—find that spot	Switch sides.
You'll feel it in the triceps—a lot	
Make sure to keep your arm by your ear	
Your hand on your elbow to help you steer	
Verse 12:	
Now cross one arm over under your chin	Do a reach-across stretch on one side.
Use your other hand to pull it in	
It's the reach-across stretch for your shoulder	
The other hand is the holder	
Verse 13:	
Now switch sides and stretch using your other arm	Switch sides.
You need to stretch both shoulders, that's the charm	
Keep your shoulder pressed down or depressed	
Keep your stretched arm over your chest	

(continued)

Lyrics	Actions
Verse 14:	
Now it's time to stretch the chest	Clasp the hands behind the chest to do a chest stretch.
Clasping hands behind your back is best	
Lift your arms as high as you can	
Keep stretching—keep to the plan	
Verse 15:	
Stretch the neck—chin over shoulder	Rotate the head so that the chin is over one shoulder.
Lack of flexibility will show when you're older	
Try to look behind—what do you see?	
Something behind you, I hope and plea	
Verse 16:	
Time to look the other way	Rotate the other way so that the chin is over the other shoulder.
Over the other shoulder and stay	
This should give you a different view	
Still looking behind you, it's true	
Verse 17:	
Increased range of motion—your flexibility	
Improves circulation—that's a probability	Inhale and raise the arms up. Exhale and lower the arms down.
Stretching will help your body recover	Alternate reaches.
You'll feel so relaxed you'll discover	
You'll feel so relaxed you'll discover	Inhale and raise the arms up. Exhale and lower the arms down.
You'll feel so relaxed	

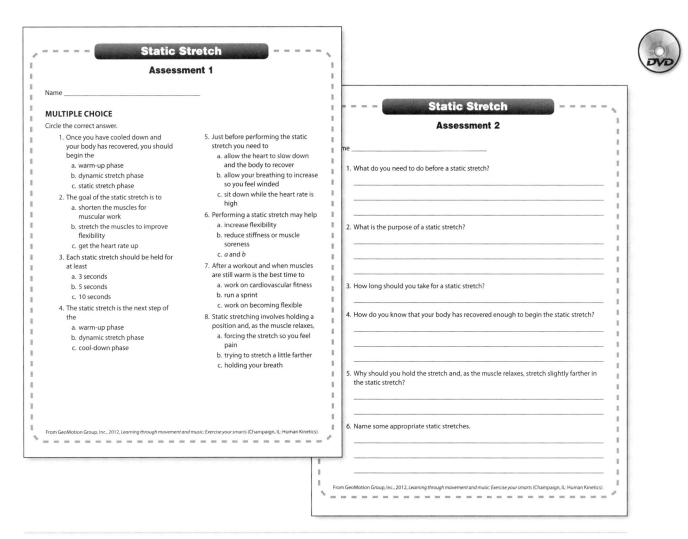

Static Stretch

Assessment 1

Name _____

MULTIPLE CHOICE

Circle the correct answer.

1. Once you have cooled down and your body has recovered, you should begin the
   a. warm-up phase
   b. dynamic stretch phase
   c. static stretch phase

2. The goal of the static stretch is to
   a. shorten the muscles for muscular work
   b. stretch the muscles to improve flexibility
   c. get the heart rate up

3. Each static stretch should be held for at least
   a. 3 seconds
   b. 5 seconds
   c. 10 seconds

4. The static stretch is the next step of the
   a. warm-up phase
   b. dynamic stretch phase
   c. cool-down phase

5. Just before performing the static stretch you need to
   a. allow the heart to slow down and the body to recover
   b. allow your breathing to increase so you feel winded
   c. sit down while the heart rate is high

6. Performing a static stretch may help
   a. increase flexibility
   b. reduce stiffness or muscle soreness
   c. *a* and *b*

7. After a workout and when muscles are still warm is the best time to
   a. work on cardiovascular fitness
   b. run a sprint
   c. work on becoming flexible

8. Static stretching involves holding a position and, as the muscle relaxes,
   a. forcing the stretch so you feel pain
   b. trying to stretch a little farther
   c. holding your breath

Static Stretch

Assessment 2

Name _____

1. What do you need to do before a static stretch?
   _____
   _____
   _____

2. What is the purpose of a static stretch?
   _____
   _____
   _____

3. How long should you take for a static stretch?
   _____

4. How do you know that your body has recovered enough to begin the static stretch?
   _____
   _____
   _____

5. Why should you hold the stretch and, as the muscle relaxes, stretch slightly farther in the static stretch?
   _____
   _____
   _____

6. Name some appropriate static stretches.
   _____
   _____
   _____
   _____

Static Stretch handouts and answer keys are available on the DVD-ROM.

INTERVAL TRAINING

Most games, sports, and physical activities are part aerobic (with oxygen) and part anaerobic (without oxygen). For example, soccer players may continuously jog or run on the field to stay in position to receive or block the ball. During the continuous jogging they are conserving their energy and have oxygen circulating throughout their bodies efficiently. That means they would be able to talk while moving on the field and be at a 7 or below on the perceived exertion scale from activity 6.

If suddenly the ball comes into a player's area, the player must use a quick burst of energy to run as fast as possible to the ball. During this quick burst of energy the player's exercise becomes anaerobic (without oxygen) and the player is at a 9 or 10 on a perceived exertion scale.

Another example of varying intensities is a tag game. While the tagger is in another area a person may jog around to try and keep a distance from the tagger. Once the chase begins, the person runs as fast as possible to prevent being tagged. During this activity both participants experience many different levels on a perceived exertion scale.

People experience varying exercise intensities in boot camp classes, too. The boot camp format is particularly effective for training people in sports that are partly aerobic and partly anaerobic (e.g., soccer and basketball).

Most athletes do interval training. That means that they alternate intensities from low, to high, to low, to high, and back to low during practice. People can experience this type of training by running a sprint as fast as possible, then walking to catch their breath, then sprinting as fast as they can again until the body forces them to slow down. This would be at a level 10 on a perceived exertion scale.

Interval training allows an athlete to work at higher intensities for longer periods of time, which leads to performing better and longer. Low-intensity exercises include jogging, fast walking, slow to moderate jumping rope, jumping jacks, and knee lifts. High-intensity exercises include sprinting, continuous fast jumping, jumping four corners quickly, and running quickly up a hill or stairs.

Lyrics and Actions to "Interval Training"

Lyrics	Actions*
Introduction:	Stand with feet together. (If using a GeoMat, stand on 1.)
Interval training's like your own boot camp	Perform a square step with a right-foot lead: Step the right foot sideward, backward, sideward, forward. (If using a GeoMat, step to 3, 9, 7, 1.) Stay on each step for 4 beats.
It can make you perform like a champ	
Alternate physical activities	
To include different intensities, oh yeah	
Verse 1:	
Fast interval:	
Let's give it a try—fast intensity	
As fast as you can—is the key	Speed up the square with 1 step for each beat. *Students can speed up even faster.*
Keep moving, moving, at a fast pace	
Pretend that you are in a race	
Keep going—don't slow down	
Keep the beat—hear your heart pound	
9 or 10 is needed on a scale	
Keep on moving—don't be a snail—oh yeah	
Keep moving, keep moving	
Now slow down—let your body recover	Slow down the square step.
You're almost breathless, you will discover	
Verse 2:	
Slow interval:	
Slow down—let your breathing get slower	
And your heart rate drops lower and lower	
Keep moving at a slower intensity	
Recuperate—you will see	
You are now working with oxygen	Do a wide march (7 and 9 on a GeoMat).
You feel better—you can even grin—oh yeah	Do a wide march again (remain on 7 and 9 on a GeoMat). Move the march forward (4 and 6 on a GeoMat) and repeat in place.
It's time to pick up the pace again—pick it up	Move the march forward (1 and 3 on a GeoMat) and repeat in place. Move the wide march backward (4 and 6 on a GeoMat).

(continued)

Lyrics	Actions
Verse 3:	
Fast interval:	
Pick it up	Move the march backward (7 and 9 on a GeoMat) and repeat. Move the march forward (4 and 6 on a GeoMat) and forward again (1 and 3 on a GeoMat).
You'll reach your anaerobic threshold	Move the march backward (4 and 6 on a GeoMat). Move the march backward (7 and 9 on a GeoMat).
Almost out of oxygen—I've been told	Continue, but speed up into a jog.
Anaerobic exercise as the aim	*Students can speed up even faster.*
To build power, strength, and muscle to your frame	
You can accomplish this task	
If you move really fast—oh yeah—moving, moving	
Verse 4:	
Slow interval:	
Now slow it down—let your body recover	Slow down the wide march backward and forward.
You're almost breathless, you will discover	
You are moving the lactic acid out	
Preparing for another high-intensity bout	
Keep your breathing at a steady pace	
You'll be able to run a marathon race	March slow with high knees.
Your energy is now replenished	
Let's do it again—we're still not finished!	
Oh no—get ready to go	
Pick it up—pick it up	Start jogging at a faster pace.
Verse 5:	
Fast interval:	*Students can speed up even faster.*
Pick it up—pick it up—fast	
Keep moving, moving at a fast pace	Face right while jogging. (If using a GeoMat, face east.)
Pretend that you are in a race	Face back while jogging. (If using a GeoMat, face south.)
Keep going—don't slow down	Face left while jogging. (If using a GeoMat, face west.)
Keep the beat—hear your heart pound	Face front while jogging. (If using a GeoMat, face north.)
Boom–boom, boom–boom	Face left while jogging. (If using a GeoMat, face west.) Turn and face right while jogging. (If using a GeoMat, face east.)
Keep moving—go, go, go	Face back while jogging. (If using a GeoMat, face south.)

Lyrics	Actions
Keep moving—go, go	Face front while jogging. (If using a GeoMat, face north.)
Verse 6:	
Slow interval:	
Slow it down—slow it down	Slow down the jog.
Slow it down—let your breathing get slower	March with knee lifts.
Your heart rate drops lower and lower	Use hands to gesture getting lower.
Slower, slower—your breathing is slower	Walk in a circle.
Lower, lower—your heart rate drops lower	
Slower and lower—lower and slower	March in place. (If using GeoMat , march on 5.)
Get ready to pick it up	
Verse 7:	*Students can speed up even faster.*
Fast interval:	
Pick it up—pick it up	Perform a marching X step with a left-foot lead. Step forward wide left, step forward wide right, step back narrow left, step back narrow right, step back wide left, step back wide right, step forward narrow left, step forward narrow right. (If using GeoMat, step 1, 3, 5, 5, 7, 9, 5, 5). Pick up the pace.
One small movement at a fast pace	
You can feel your heart race	
Your breathing and heart rate are getting louder	
When you finish—you can't feel much prouder	
Hear your heart—ba-boom, ba-boom	
Hear your breath—ha ha, ha ha	
Hear your heart—ba-boom, ba-boom	Perform a jumping X. Jump both feet forward wide, jump both feet back narrow, jump both feet backward wide, jump both feet forward narrow. Put the arms in front of the heart and pulse them in and out to mimic the heart beating. (If using a GeoMat, jump 1 and 3, 5, 7 and 9, 5.)
Hear your breath—ha ha, ha ha	
Verse 8:	
Slow interval:	
Now slower—ba-boom, ba-boom	Slow down the jumping X step.
And slower—ha ha, ha ha	
One more time you're getting slower	Do marching knee lifts in place. (If using GeoMat, march on 5.)
And bringing your heart rate lower	
Go slower, slower—your heart rate's lower, lower	Walk in a circle. Use hands to gesture getting lower.

(continued)

Lyrics and Actions to "Interval Training" *(continued)*

Lyrics	Actions
Ending:	
Interval training's like your own boot camp	March in place. (If using a GeoMat, march on 5.)
It can make you perform like a champ	
Build strength and muscle mass	Do alternating heel lifts in place. (If using a GeoMat, do heel lifts on 5.)
Any fitness test you will pass	

*The first time they participate, have students use a right-foot lead, then next time have them try a left-foot lead to balance out the body.

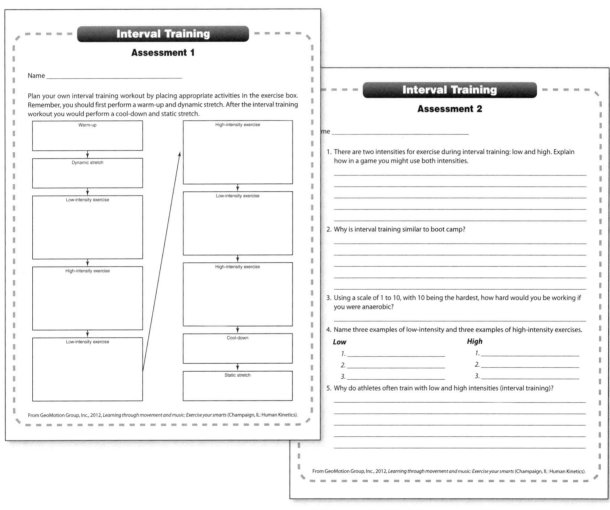

Interval Training handouts and an answer key for Interval Training Assessment 2 are available on the DVD-ROM. Each student will create a personal interval training flow chart in Interval Training Assessment 1, so you will need to examine each one separately.

FITNESS TEST

A fitness test is a great way to measure individual health and fitness and find out how those measurements compare to fitness standards. That knowledge helps determine what areas need improvement.

Because most students take physical education classes in school, schools often provide fitness testing. Schools offer some tests that you may have heard of or taken. The most widely known are the President's Challenge and Fitnessgram. Students and teachers can use the information learned from the fitness test to help set individual goals for improvement.

Most fitness tests provide feedback on health-related fitness components. Four tests in this book go with the lyrics to *Fitness Test* (see the Components of Health-Related Fitness poster on page 60). These are easy tests to deliver and students can chart their own scores. They can make goals based on their scores and see if they show improvement with future tests.

- The back-saver sit-and-reach test measures flexibility in the lower back and hamstrings.
- Jump four corners measures cardiovascular endurance.
- Plank shoulder touches measure muscular strength. In plank shoulder touch, the student gets into a push-up or modified push-up position. The student then lifts one hand to touch the opposite shoulder, returns to the starting position, and repeats the move, alternating sides until time is up.
- Curl-ups measure muscular endurance.

Obesity levels have risen in children and adults over the past 30 years (CDC, 2011a, 2011b; Villaire, n.d.; WHO Consultation on Obesity, 1999). Compounding this problem is that fitness levels are also declining (CDC, 2010; Brownson, et al., 2005; Villaire, n.d.). Therefore, more of a focus is being placed on fitness testing and improving fitness. Fitness facilities offer testing so that personal trainers can provide better workouts to meet client needs.

Fitness testing is for the individual to strive for improvement. It may be fun to compete and compare oneself to others, but it's more productive to focus on oneself.

After students have taken the fitness test once, they should continue working out, especially in the areas that need work according to the test results. Then, have students try testing again in a month or so. It can be inspiring for students to show improved performance.

Lyrics and Actions to "Fitness Test"

The movements described in this table can be done entirely by the students so that they get some practice doing the movement before they take the test. You can also split the time between yourself and the students, as shown in the video, so that you can demonstrate the tests and then have students take their turn. Please note that you may need to pause the video if equipment sharing is necessary, as may be the case in the back-saver sit-and-reach test.

Lyrics	Actions*
Verse 1:	
Why take a fitness test? you might ask	Hold the hands out wide in a *why* gesture.
To know where to improve and plan your tasks	Point to the head and gesture down the body.
The test is for you—you compete with yourself	Point to "you" twice (on the first *you* and on *yourself*).
Your main goal—improve your health	Flex the biceps muscles and gesture down the body.
Measure your fitness with a four-part test	Flex the biceps muscles and then hold up four fingers.
You can repeat to see your progress	
Try this test to know your score	Wave with an inviting gesture.
Then set goals—know where to do more	
Verse 2:	
A sit and reach shows flexibility in the back	Point to the back.
It's an easy test—give it a whack	
Sit with one leg bent, the other in front of you	Get in position for the sit-and-reach test.
See how far you can reach toward your shoe	
Use a ruler to calculate a score	Gesture getting measuring tape, stick in position.
Repeat more than once—try reaching more	
Give it a try—sit and reach	
Use correct form—that I preach	
First try—sitting tall	Reach.
Now you reach—give it your all	
Stretch and reach—reach some more	Repeat the reach.
Down to the inch—see your score	
Now press Pause—record your best score	
Press Play when ready to do some more	
Verse 3:	
For cardio see how many times you can jump	Look and point at the four squares they are to jump.
Four corners of a square—for 30 seconds in a lump	

Lyrics	Actions
Land with two feet—bend your knees to land	
Use your arms to propel you is a good plan	
Ready—Go	
Music provides 30-second countdown.	Jump forward, right, backward, and left. (If using a GeoMat, jump 1,3,9,7.) *Students may change direction about halfway through.*
Now press Pause—record your score	
Press Play when ready to do some more	
Verse 4:	
For muscular strength—get in push-up position	Get into a push-up or modified push-up position.
From your toes or your knees—that is the tradition	Make sure to have a straight line between the knees and shoulders (no bending at the hips).
Touch your shoulder with one hand—then you switch	Practice touching the right hand to the left shoulder and the left hand to the right shoulder.
Do as many as you can without a hitch	
Test your strength in your arms and chest	
Give it a try—do your best	
Perform for 30 seconds—count each time you touch	
Don't you worry—if you can't do much	
Ready—go	
Music provides 30-second countdown.	Perform as many touches as you can in 30 seconds while keeping good form.
Now press Pause—record your score	
Press Play when ready to do some more	
Verse 5:	
For muscular endurance turn over and sit	Sit down.
For abdominal curl-ups—how many can you get?	
Lie on your back—knees are bent	Lie down on the back with the knees bent and feet on the floor.
Place arms by your side—I give my consent	Place the arms parallel to the ground.
Curl your rib cage and reach with fingertips	Try a practice curl-up by contracting the abdominals and lifting the upper back and shoulders off the floor.
At least 3 inches—count how many trips	*Use a guide on the floor (a bean bag may work) to ensure that the participant reaches forward 3 inches (7.62 cm).*
Perform for 30 seconds—count each time you glide	
Remember, 3 inches is your guide	
Ready—go	

(continued)

Lyrics	Actions
Music provides 30-second countdown.	Perform as many repetitions as possible in 30 seconds with good form.
Now press Pause—record your score	
Press Play when ready to do some more	
Break:	
Catch your breath—it's time to rest	
I know you did your best	
You have completed all four	
Time to calculate your score	
Ending:	
Look at your info—for all four	
Now it's time to self-assess	
Know your fitness—you don't have to guess	
Keep a log—record your scores	
See if you've improved from before	
Peace out	
You're done	

*A 30-second count will be used to help participants know how long they have left. Use this time to encourage students, make sure they have correct form, and have them or their partners count the number of repetitions.

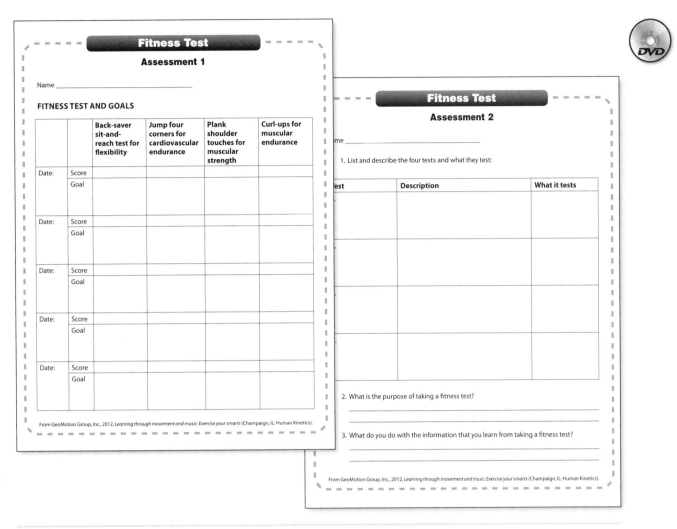

Fitness Test

Assessment 1

Name _____

FITNESS TEST AND GOALS

		Back-saver sit-and-reach test for flexibility	Jump four corners for cardiovascular endurance	Plank shoulder touches for muscular strength	Curl-ups for muscular endurance
Date:	Score				
	Goal				
Date:	Score				
	Goal				
Date:	Score				
	Goal				
Date:	Score				
	Goal				
Date:	Score				
	Goal				

Fitness Test

Assessment 2

Name _____

1. List and describe the four tests and what they test:

Test	Description	What it tests

2. What is the purpose of taking a fitness test?

_____

_____

3. What do you do with the information that you learn from taking a fitness test?

_____

_____

Fitness Test handouts and an answer key for Fitness Test Assessment 2 are available on the DVD-ROM.

11

I'VE BEEN WORKING ON MY BODY

Components of Health-Related Fitness

The song *I've Been Working on My Body* provides information about health-related components of fitness. Health-related fitness is linked to fitness components that may lower risks such as high blood pressure, diabetes, or low-back pain. Health-related physical fitness includes the following components:

- Flexibility—ability to move joints through their proper range of motion
- Cardiovascular endurance—ability of the heart and lungs to deliver blood to muscles
- Muscular strength and endurance—strong enough to do normal activities easily and protect the low back
    - Muscular strength—ability of the muscles to exert a single maximal force to overcome resistance
    - Muscular endurance—ability of the muscles to maintain continuous force over a period of time
- Body composition—ratio or percent of lean body mass and body fat. Lean body mass is the weight of the body minus body fat. Everyone must have some essential fat, but too much body fat, especially around the waist, leads to higher health risks.

Some experts say that there are four components of fitness. They combine muscular strength and endurance as one component, whereas others keep them separate and show five components. Each health component contributes to a healthy quality of life and is important to a person's well-being. Optimal physical fitness is a combination of lifestyle, nutrition, and habits, but it cannot be reached without an appropriate level of physical activity and without maintaining the health components of fitness.

In physical fitness, body composition is used to describe the percentages of fat, bone, and muscle in human bodies. Most doctors use a table that shows a person's height and weight to estimate body composition or how much of his or her body is fat. Since muscular tissue takes up less space in the body than fat tissue, it is often hard to tell without sophisticated equipment how much true body fat a person may have. Two people at the same height and same body weight may look completely different from each other because they have a different body composition. A person needs to be able to tell what is inside: Is the weight fat or is it muscle?

One of the best things people can do to keep their bodies lean and fit is to exercise to burn calories. They must also consume healthy foods to keep a good balance of lean body mass versus body fat.

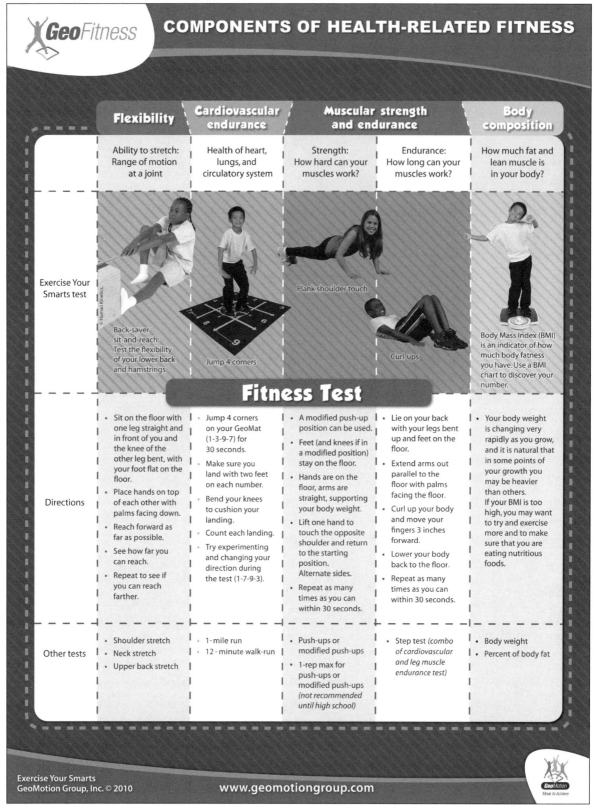

COMPONENTS OF HEALTH-RELATED FITNESS

GeoFitness

	Flexibility	Cardiovascular endurance	Muscular strength and endurance		Body composition
	Ability to stretch: Range of motion at a joint	Health of heart, lungs, and circulatory system	Strength: How hard can your muscles work?	Endurance: How long can your muscles work?	How much fat and lean muscle is in your body?
Exercise Your Smarts test	Back-saver sit-and-reach: Test the flexibility of your lower back and hamstrings	Jump 4 corners	Plank shoulder touch	Curl-ups	Body Mass Index (BMI) is an indicator of how much body fatness you have. Use a BMI chart to discover your number.

Fitness Test

	Flexibility	Cardiovascular endurance	Muscular strength and endurance		Body composition
Directions	• Sit on the floor with one leg straight and in front of you and the knee of the other leg bent, with your foot flat on the floor. • Place hands on top of each other with palms facing down. • Reach forward as far as possible. • See how far you can reach. • Repeat to see if you can reach farther.	• Jump 4 corners on your GeoMat (1-3-9-7) for 30 seconds. • Make sure you land with two feet on each number. • Bend your knees to cushion your landing. • Count each landing. • Try experimenting and changing your direction during the test (1-7-9-3).	• A modified push-up position can be used. • Feet (and knees if in a modified position) stay on the floor. • Hands are on the floor, arms are straight, supporting your body weight. • Lift one hand to touch the opposite shoulder and return to the starting position. Alternate sides. • Repeat as many times as you can within 30 seconds.	• Lie on your back with your legs bent up and feet on the floor. • Extend arms out parallel to the floor with palms facing the floor. • Curl up your body and move your fingers 3 inches forward. • Lower your body back to the floor. • Repeat as many times as you can within 30 seconds.	• Your body weight is changing very rapidly as you grow, and it is natural that in some points of your growth you may be heavier than others. If your BMI is too high, you may want to try and exercise more and to make sure that you are eating nutritious foods.
Other tests	• Shoulder stretch • Neck stretch • Upper back stretch	• 1-mile run • 12-minute walk-run	• Push-ups or modified push-ups • 1-rep max for push-ups or modified push-ups *(not recommended until high school)*	• Step test *(combo of cardiovascular and leg muscle endurance test)*	• Body weight • Percent of body fat

Exercise Your Smarts
GeoMotion Group, Inc. © 2010

www.geomotiongroup.com

GeoMotion Move to Achieve

This poster, found on the DVD-ROM, helps students remember the different areas of health-related fitness and how to test themselves in them.

Lyrics and Actions to "I've Been Working on My Body: Components of Fitness"

Lyrics	Actions*
Introduction:	
I've been working on my body	Bring one arm up to show the biceps muscle.
I've been working on my body	Bring the other arm up to show the biceps muscle. Bring the elbows together and return to showing the biceps muscles.
I've been working on my body	Continue to bring the elbows together and return to showing the biceps muscles.
Using health components	Touch alternating elbows to the knees with a wide march.
I've been working on my body	
Because it makes sense	
Verse 1:	
Flexibility	Alternate reaches.
Cardiovascular	Show the heart pumping.
Muscular strength—endurance	Show the biceps muscles; do overhead presses.
Body composition	Move the hands from head to toes.
Work my body, work, work my body	Bring one arm up to show the biceps muscle, then bring the other arm up to show the biceps muscle. Bring the elbows together and return to showing the biceps muscles.
Work my body, work, work my body	Continue to bring the elbows together and return to showing the biceps muscles.
Verse 2:	
Bend and stretch—bend and stretch	Squat with the hands on the thighs, then straighten the legs reaching both arms up.
Flexibility	
Heart rate up—run, work out	Show the heart pumping and jog.
Cardiovascular	
Muscular strength—endurance	Show the biceps muscles and do overhead presses.
Body composition	Move the hands from head to toes.
Verse 3:	
Muscular strength and endurance	Show the biceps muscles; do overhead presses.
Makes you stronger each day	
Body composition	Move the hands from head to toes; raise the hands overhead.
Keeps you lean—keeps fat away	Press one hand out; press the other hand out.
Verse 4:	
When you work your body	Pretend to have weights: Go to the floor, then reach overhead.
With health components	
Work your body	
Because it makes sense	Bring one arm up to show the biceps muscle, then bring the other arm up to show the biceps muscle.

*Have students try this combination first with a right-foot lead, then with a left-foot lead to balance out the body.

I've Been Working on My Body: Components of Health-Related Fitness

Assessment 1

Name _____

COMPONENTS OF HEALTH-RELATED FITNESS

Unscramble the terms related to the components of health-related fitness below.

1. fyilbleitxi _____

2. nlae _____

3. ivcacrsualroda _____

4. uuamsrlc _____

5. nercuneda _____

6. thaer _____

7. htgstenr _____

8. dbyo otnpmoiosci _____

9. hthela _____

10. ocpmnonest _____

From GeoMotion Group, Inc., 2012, *Learning through movement and music: Exercise your smarts* (Champaign, IL: Human Kinetics).

I've Been Working on My Body: Components of Health-Related Fitness

Assessment 2

Name _____

1. List the components of health-related fitness.

_____
_____
_____
_____
_____

2. What are the activities or exercises you might perform to work on your health-related components?

_____
_____
_____
_____
_____

3. Define the term *body composition*.

_____
_____
_____
_____
_____

4. Why is it hard to get adequate information about your body composition?

_____
_____
_____
_____
_____
_____

From GeoMotion Group, Inc., 2012, *Learning through movement and music: Exercise your smarts* (Champaign, IL: Human Kinetics).

I've Been Working on My Body handouts and answer keys are available on the DVD-ROM.

BOOGIE WOOGIE BONE DANCE

The human skeleton consists of 206 bones. People are actually born with more bones (about 300), but many fuse together as they grow up. The femur (upper leg) is the largest bone of the body. The skeleton has many important functions.

Support

The skeleton provides the framework that supports the body and maintains its shape. Without the skeleton, a person would look like one big bowl of gelatin and would not be able to stand or move. The pelvis, ligaments, and muscles provide a floor for the pelvic structures where many vital organs sit. Without the ribs, cartilage, and muscles, the lungs would collapse.

Movement

Bones are connected to other bones at joints. The joints between bones allow movement. Movement is powered by skeletal muscles, which are attached to the skeleton at different sites on bones. Muscles, bones, and joints provide the main mechanics for movement, all coordinated by the nervous system.

Protection

The skeleton protects many vital organs:

- The skull protects the brain, the eyes, and the middle and inner ears.
- The vertebrae protect the spinal cord.
- The rib cage, spine, and sternum protect the lungs, heart, and major blood vessels.
- The spine protects the digestive system.

Blood Cell Production

The skeleton is the site where blood cells are produced, which takes place in red bone marrow. Marrow is found in the center of long bones.

Storage

Bones store calcium (a mineral found in many foods such as milk, broccoli, leafy greens, tofu, canned salmon, and other foods). Calcium is an important component of a healthy diet and a mineral necessary for life. Bones also manufacture and store other important minerals.

BONES

GeoFitness

FRONT

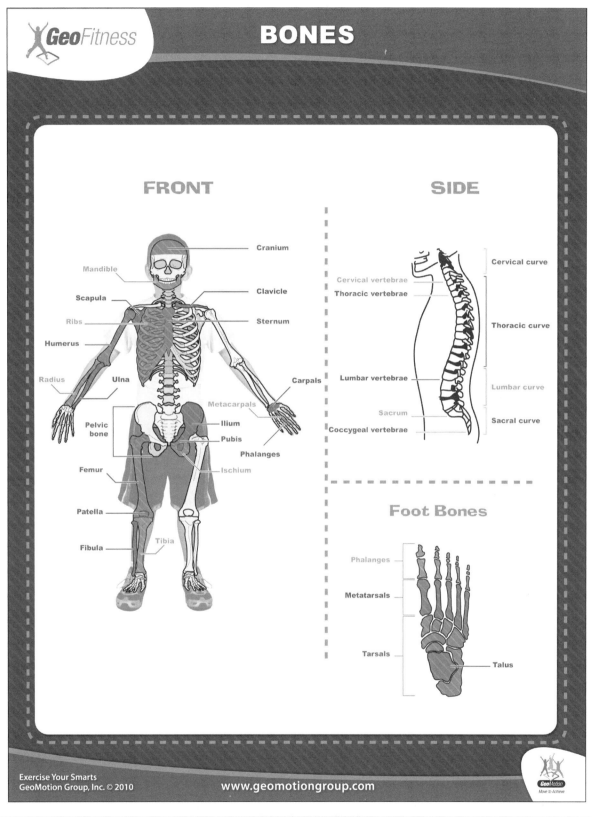

Cranium

Mandible

Scapula

Clavicle

Ribs

Sternum

Humerus

Radius

Ulna

Carpals

Metacarpals

Pelvic bone

Ilium

Pubis

Phalanges

Femur

Ischium

Patella

Fibula

Tibia

SIDE

Cervical curve

Cervical vertebrae

Thoracic vertebrae

Thoracic curve

Lumbar vertebrae

Lumbar curve

Sacrum

Sacral curve

Coccygeal vertebrae

Foot Bones

Phalanges

Metatarsals

Tarsals

Talus

Use the poster found on the DVD-ROM to teach students where many of their bones are located. The poster includes a side view of the vertebrae.

Lyrics and Actions to "Boogie Woogie Bone Dance"

Lyrics	Actions
Introduction:	
B-bone-bones	Swing both arms back and forth.
B-bone-bones	
Chorus:	
Boogie woogie, boogie woogie bones	Swing both arms right and left, then around in a circle in front of the body.
Boogie woogie, boogie woogie bones	Swing both arms right and left, then around in a circle in front of the body.
Bones bones bones, boogie woogie bones	Swing the arms right and left. Move low then return to standing tall.
Verse 1:	
Touch your cranium, the big bone in your head—oh yeah	Tap the head.
Move your hand and touch your mandible instead	Tap the jaw.
We're gonna work the vertebrae	Tap back spine area.
Point to each bone that I say	
Cervical—boogie bones, thoracic—boogie bones	Tap the top of the back.
Lumbar—boogie bones, sacrum—boogie bones	Continue tapping as you move down the spine area.
Coccyx—boogie bones	
Those are the bones in your vertebrae!	
Repeat Chorus.	
Verse 2:	
Touch your sternum—right there in your chest—oh yeah	Tap the sternum.
Touch your ribs—make them contract, then rest	Place the hands on the ribs and take in a deep breath showing the hands moving.
Scapula—shoulder blade—this is fun—it's not a test	Tap the shoulder blades.
Find your vertebrae—boogie bones	Tap the spine area (vertebrae).
Go below—boogie bones	Gesture to lower body.
That's your pelvis—boogie bones	Tap the pelvis (hip area).
You should know—boogie bones	Point to head, then swing the arms.
B-bone-bones	
Verse 3:	
Touch your humerus at your arm's top	Tap the humerus (top arm bone).
Next is the radius but this boogie doesn't stop—oh yeah	Tap the radius (lower arm bone on the same side as the thumb).
Find the ulna, now to the hand we'll drop	Tap the ulna (lower arm bone on the same side as the pinkie finger).

(continued)

Lyrics	Actions
Carpals—boogie bones; metacarpals—boogie bones	Point to the carpals (bones in the wrist area), then the metacarpals (bones in the hand).
Phalanges—boogie bones; boogie bones—boogie bones	Point to the phalanges (bones in the fingers) and then wiggle the fingers.
These are bones in your hand	
Just making sure you understand	Swing the arms right and left and then point to the brain.
Repeat Chorus.	
Verse 4:	
The top of your leg has the femur bone, that's true	Tap the femur (big upper leg bone).
The patella is your knee—and there are two	Tap the knees.
The tibia and fibula and the leg is through	Tap the tibia (lower leg bone on the same side as the big toe), then point to the fibula (lower leg bone that is on the same side as the pinkie toe).
Boogie bones in your feet, boogie bones in your feet	Swing the arms right and left.
Talus—boogie bones; tarsals—boogie bones	Tap the talus (bone in the heel area); tap the tarsals (bones in the top of the foot near the ankle).
Metatarsals in your feet, too—the boogie woogie bone dance is almost through!	Tap the metatarsals (bones in the middle of the top of the foot).
Ending:	
Shake, shake, shake—boogie woogie bones	Shake the arms overhead, then shake low.
Shake, shake, shake—boogie woogie bones	Shake the arms overhead, then shake low.
Bones, bones, bones—boogie woogie bones	Continue to shake low, then stand.

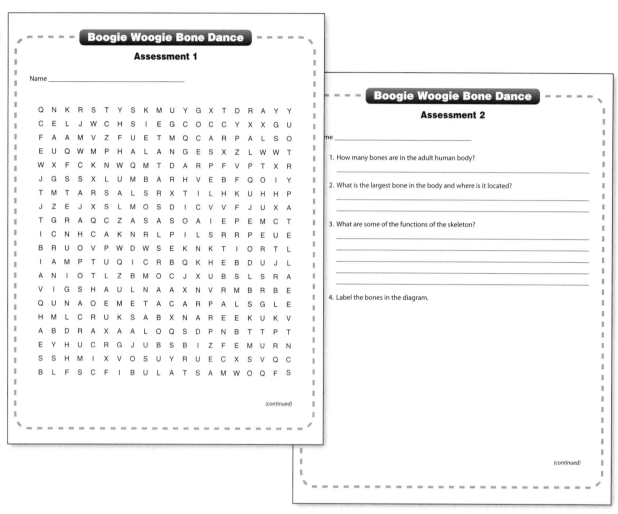

Boogie Woogie Bone Dance

Assessment 1

Name _____

```
Q  N  K  R  S  T  Y  S  K  M  U  Y  G  X  T  D  R  A  Y  Y
C  E  L  J  W  C  H  S  I  E  G  C  O  C  C  Y  X  X  G  U
F  A  A  M  V  Z  F  U  E  T  M  Q  C  A  R  P  A  L  S  O
E  U  Q  W  M  P  H  A  L  A  N  G  E  S  X  Z  L  W  W  T
W  X  F  C  K  N  W  Q  M  T  D  A  R  P  F  V  P  T  X  R
J  G  S  S  X  L  U  M  B  A  R  H  V  E  B  F  Q  O  I  Y
T  M  T  A  R  S  A  L  S  R  X  T  I  L  H  K  U  H  H  P
J  Z  E  J  X  S  L  M  O  S  D  I  C  V  V  F  J  U  X  A
T  G  R  A  Q  C  Z  A  S  A  S  O  A  I  E  P  E  M  C  T
I  C  N  H  C  A  K  N  R  L  P  I  L  S  R  R  P  E  U  E
B  R  U  O  V  P  W  D  W  S  E  K  N  K  T  I  O  R  T  L
I  A  M  P  T  U  Q  I  C  R  B  Q  K  H  E  B  D  U  J  L
A  N  I  O  T  L  Z  B  M  O  C  J  X  U  B  S  L  S  R  A
V  I  G  S  H  A  U  L  N  A  A  X  N  V  R  M  B  R  B  E
Q  U  N  A  O  E  M  E  T  A  C  A  R  P  A  L  S  G  L  E
H  M  L  C  R  U  K  S  A  B  X  N  A  R  E  E  K  U  K  V
A  B  D  R  A  X  A  A  L  O  Q  S  D  P  N  B  T  T  P  T
E  Y  H  U  C  R  G  J  U  B  S  B  I  Z  F  E  M  U  R  N
S  S  H  M  I  X  V  O  S  U  Y  R  U  E  C  X  S  V  Q  C
B  L  F  S  C  F  I  B  U  L  A  T  S  A  M  W  O  Q  F  S
```

(continued)

Boogie Woogie Bone Dance

Assessment 2

Name _____

1. How many bones are in the adult human body?
   _____

2. What is the largest bone in the body and where is it located?
   _____
   _____

3. What are some of the functions of the skeleton?
   _____
   _____
   _____
   _____
   _____

4. Label the bones in the diagram.

(continued)

Boogie Woogie Bone Dance handouts and answer keys are available on the DVD-ROM.

WHY DO WE EXERCISE?

The benefits to exercise are numerous. Longevity is one benefit. Longevity means life expectancy, or how long a person will live. People who exercise can expect to live longer and have a better quality of life.

Exercise reduces the chances of disease or disability by preventing type 2 diabetes, strengthening the heart and lungs, building bone density, keeping muscles strong, lowering cholesterol and risk of heart attack, and improving circulation. Exercise also boosts oxygen levels in the blood, which stimulates collagen production. Collagen is part of the lymphatic system, which helps removes toxins from the body.

Mental health benefits include lowering stress, releasing endorphins that enhance a person's mood, and increasing confidence and self-esteem.

Other benefits include increased energy, weight management, peak efficiency at work, enhancement of brain functioning, and increased concentration.

People have many types of exercise to choose from. It is each person's responsibility to make good, healthy choices and find enjoyable activities.

This song provides a lot of information as to why everyone should exercise. Ask students how many different reasons they can count to exercise.

Lyrics and Actions to "Why Do We Exercise?"

Lyrics	Actions
Chorus:	Stand in a wide stance. (If using a GeoMat, place the feet on 7 and 9.)
Why? Why? Why? Why? Why do we exercise?	Hold the arms out to the sides and lift in a "Why?" motion; do alternating arm curls.
Why? Why? Why? Why? Why do we exercise?	Repeat.
Verse 1:	
Exercise is the key to healthy longevity	Do lunges with arm curls.
For any age or ability—it's your responsibility	Move forward with lunges.
Exercise helps increase energy—oh yeah	Do narrow marches moving backward. (If using a GeoMat, march to 8.)
Body works at peak efficiency—oh yeah	Move forward with lunges.
Energy for daily tasks and work is really a great perk	Do narrow marches moving backward. (If using a GeoMat, march to 8.)
Exer—Exer—Exercise	Do a supported bend with hands on knees or a rounded back, then straighten back with a jump.
Repeat Chorus.	
Verse 2:	
Exercise combats disease like type 2 diabetes	Rock step 3 times. (If using a GeoMat, rock step on 4 and 8.)
Lowers cholesterol, reduces plaque—lowers risk of heart attack	Rock step 3 times. (If using a GeoMat, rock step on 6 and 8.)
Exercise strengthens your heart and lungs—oh yeah	Rock step 3 times. (If using a GeoMat, rock step on 4 and 8.)
Improves circulation and keeps you feeling young—oh yeah	Rock step 3 times. (If using a GeoMat, rock step on 6 and 8.)
Exercise helps manage your weight—being heavy doesn't have to be your fate	Rock step 3 times. (If using a GeoMat, rock step on 4 and 8.)
Exer—Exer—Exercise	Rock step 1 time. (If using a GeoMat, rock step on 6 and 8.) Do a supported bend with hands on knees or a rounded back, then straighten back with a jump.
Repeat Chorus.	
Verse 3:	
Exercise lowers stress—more confidence you will possess	March wide. (If using a GeoMat, march on 7 and 9.) March wide while moving forward. (If using a GeoMat, march wide on 4 and 6.)
Take the stairs—walk more—play outside—help with a chore	March wide while moving forward. (If using a GeoMat, march on 1 and 3.) Jump narrow. (If using a GeoMat, jump on 2.) Jump back. (If using a GeoMat, jump to 8.)
Improves your mood with endorphins—oh yeah	March wide. (If using a GeoMat, march on 7 and 9.) March wide while moving forward. (If using a GeoMat, march on 4 and 6.)

Lyrics	Actions
They make you feel happy and grin—oh yeah	March wide while moving forward. (If using a GeoMat, march on 1 and 3.) Jump narrow. (If using a GeoMat, jump on 2.) Jump back. (If using a GeoMat, jump to 8.)
Boosting your self-esteem while you're able to blow off steam	March wide. (If using a GeoMat, march on 7 and 9.) March wide while moving forward. (If using a GeoMat, march on 4 and 6.)
Exer—Exer—Exercise	March wide while moving forward. (If using a GeoMat, march on 1 and 3.) Jump narrow. (If using a GeoMat, jump to 2.) Jump back. (If using a GeoMat, jump to 8.)
Verse 4:	
Exercise increases blood flow	Walk in a circle.
Speeds up messages from cell to cell	
Builds better concentration—helps you learn very well	Change direction and walk in a circle again.
Weight-bearing exercise builds bone density—keeps muscles strong	March wide. (If using a GeoMat, march on 7 and 9.)
Helps you sleep—with exercise and nutrition you can't go wrong	March wide while moving forward. (If using a GeoMat, march on 4 and 6.) March wide while moving forward. (If using a GeoMat, march on 1 and 3.)
Repeat Chorus.	Do wide jumps backward. (If using a GeoMat, jump on 1 and 3, 4 and 6, 7 and 9.) Hold the arms out to the sides and lift in a "Why?" motion; do alternating arm curls.
Verse 5:	
Exercise helps with better skin, boosts circulation and oxygen	Show biceps muscles, perform overhead presses, and bring the elbows together.
Increases production of collagen that would remove a toxin	Alternate touching elbows to knees.
Exercise should be fun—oh yeah	
Benefits can't be undone—oh yeah	Alternate straight-leg toe touches.
Find something you enjoy for every girl or boy	Show movements for biking, jumping rope, and using a pogo stick.
Exer—Exer—Exercise—Exercise!	Jump wide and show the biceps muscles. Do overhead presses and show biceps muscles.

Why Do We Exercise?

Assessment 1

Name _____

Complete the sentence to show your knowledge of the benefits of exercise. You can often use rhyming words in the sentences to give you a hint to the correct answer. You can also play the music to the song to help you determine the correct answers.

1. Exercise is the _____ to healthy longevity.

2. It's your job or _____.

3. Exercise is for any age or _____.

4. Exercise helps _____ energy.

5. Exercise helps your body work at peak _____.

6. Exercise combats diseases such as type 2 _____.

7. Exercise lowers cholesterol, reduces plaque, and lowers risk of _____ attack.

8. Exercise strengthens your heart and _____.

9. Exercise improves circulation and keeps you feeling _____.

10. Exercise helps manage your _____.

11. Being heavy does not have to be your _____.

12. Exercise helps lower _____. More confidence you will possess.

13. Exercise improves your _____ with endorphins.

14. They make you feel happy and _____.

15. Exercise boosts your self-_____ while you're able to blow off steam.

(continued)

Why Do We Exercise?

Assessment 2

Name _____

1. Many people say you need to develop the whole person—mentally, physically, and emotionally. Place each benefit of exercise in the appropriate category in the following table.

Benefits of Exercise

Physical and health benefits of exercise	Mental and emotional benefits of exercise

2. Why do you think it's important for exercise to be fun?

_____
_____
_____
_____

3. Why should you exercise?

_____
_____
_____
_____
_____

Why Do We Exercise? handouts and answer keys are available on the DVD-ROM.

FITT PRINCIPLE

The FITT principle is a set of guidelines that help a person get the most out of workouts. FITT stands for the following:

- Frequency—how often a person exercises
- Intensity—how hard a person works during exercise
- Time—how long a person exercises
- Type—what type of activity the person performs

A person can change these aspects of an exercise program and, in fact, should do so regularly to avoid boredom and stay fit. For example, if a person starts out walking three times a week for 30 minutes at a moderate pace, weight loss and increased endurance may result at the beginning, but after a few weeks of the same workouts, the body will adapt.

Some possible workout changes for this person include the following:

- Change in frequency: Add another day of walking.
- Change in intensity: Walk faster or add some running.
- Change in time: Walk for a longer period of time.
- Change in type: Try something different such as swimming or cycling.

FITT PRINCIPLE

GeoFitness

	FREQUENCY	**INTENSITY**	**TIME**	**TYPE**
	How often	How hard	How long	Exercise type
General exercise	• Daily	• All activity counts—from low to vigorous intensity	• Accumulative 60 minutes	• Fitness activities • Games • Play • Chores
Flexibility	• Daily • Before and after exercise	• Slow and controlled movement	• 10–60 seconds per stretch	• Dynamic stretches • Static stretches
Cardiovascular endurance (aerobic)	• 3–5 times/wk	• Moderate to vigorous intensity • 6–8 on perceived exertion scales • 60%–85% of maximum heart rate	• 30–60 minutes	• Continuous aerobic activity • Break into a sweat and still be able to talk • Activities include: *fast walking, jogging, biking, jumping rope, swimming, dancing*
Muscular endurance	• Alternate days • 3 times/wk	• Low to moderate resistance	• 10–20 repetitions • 3 sets	• Best to begin with body weight
Muscular strength	• Alternate days • 3 times/wk	• Moderate resistance	• 8–12 repetitions • 1–3 sets	• Body weight • Resistance bands • Handheld weights • Weighted balls
Body composition	• 5–7 times/wk	• Combination of intensities	• Dependent on intensity and type of exercise	• Aerobic • Anaerobic • Interval training • Resistance training
Anaerobic	• Alternate days • 2–3 times/wk	• 9 or 10 on perceived exertion scale • 90% of maximum heart rate	• 2–3 minutes per activity session	• Sprinting • Jumping • Quick feet

Exercise Your Smarts
GeoMotion Group, Inc. © 2010

www.geomotiongroup.com

GeoMotion
Move to Achieve

This poster, found on the DVD-ROM, breaks down the FITT principle and educates students on the recommendations for each part.

Lyrics and Actions to "FITT Principle"

Lyrics	Actions
Chorus 1:	
F-I-T-T	Make F-I-T-T with the arms (as with "YMCA"); use slow repetition.
F-I-T-T	Make a fast F-I-T-T.
FITT principle	Place the hands on the hips.
Verse 1:	
Frequency, intensity, time, and type	Make a slow F-I-T-T.
Helps with exercise—that's no hype	Place the hands on the hips.
Chorus 2:	
F-I-T-T	Make a fast F-I-T-T.
It's the key	Signal the thumbs up.
FITT principle	Place the hands on the hips.
Verse 2:	
F is for frequency—how often or many	Make a letter F with the arms. Count on the fingers of one hand, then the other hand.
Over your lifetime you'll work out plenty	Do arm curls to the sides.
I is for intensity—how hard or tough	Make a letter I with the body, then do fast arm curls to the front.
Do you have the right stuff?	Do slow arm curls to the front.
FITT principle	Place the hands on the hips.
T is for time of duration—how long	Make a letter T, then tap the wrist to indicate a watch.
30 to 60 minutes of cardio—makes your heart strong	Make a circle over the wrist to indicate time passing on a watch, then show the heart pumping.
T is for type—or activity of choice	Make the letter T with the arms and the body. Jog.
If you pick the right activity you will rejoice	
Repeat Chorus 1.	
I want to give you more information	Step tap side to side. (If using a GeoMat, step tap on 4 and 6.) Point to the head.
This knowledge will give you a better foundation	Continue step taps.
Repeat Chorus 2.	
Verse 3:	
Frequency's how many sessions each week	Stand in a wide stance and alternate arm reaches.
Most days is what you seek	
Cardio, endurance, strength, and flexibility	Do step taps side to side with punches.
All are important—it's your responsibility	

(continued)

Lyrics and Actions to "FITT Principle" *(continued)*

Lyrics	Actions
Verse 4:	
To find out intensity—that's how hard	Alternate knees up while arms pull down.
Keep perceived exertion—on a card	
10 is the hardest and 1 is at rest	
When working out at 7 or 8 it's the best	
Repeat Chorus 1.	
Verse 5:	
Time is important—it can vary, that's okay	Tap the wrist to indicate a watch.
Take 30 to 60 minutes each day	March.
Type of activity gives you lots of selections	Make a T with the arms.
Variety may reduce your objections	Jog.
Swimming, biking, football, dance	Show motions for swimming, biking, throwing a football, and dance.
Try different things—take a chance	Continue to dance, then do jumping jacks.
Repeat Chorus 1.	
Ending:	
F-I-T-T will help you remember	Make a fast F-I-T-T. Point to the head.
From January through December	
F-I-T-T	Make a fast F-I-T-T.
FITT principle	Place the hands on the hips.
F-I-T-T	Make a fast F-I-T-T.
FITT principle	Place the hands on the hips.

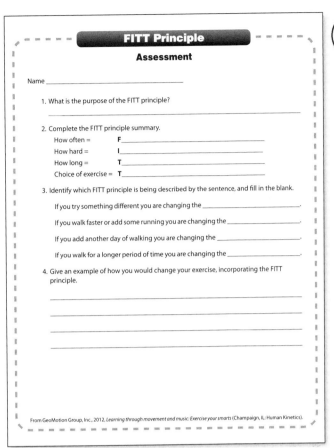

FITT Principle

Assessment

Name _____

1. What is the purpose of the FITT principle?

   _____

2. Complete the FITT principle summary.

   How often =   F_____

   How hard =   I_____

   How long =   T_____

   Choice of exercise = T_____

3. Identify which FITT principle is being described by the sentence, and fill in the blank.

   If you try something different you are changing the _____.

   If you walk faster or add some running you are changing the _____.

   If you add another day of walking you are changing the _____.

   If you walk for a longer period of time you are changing the _____.

4. Give an example of how you would change your exercise, incorporating the FITT principle.

   _____

   _____

   _____

   _____

   _____

The FITT Principle handout and answer key are available on the DVD-ROM.

References

American Academy of Pediatrics. (2011). Combining physical activity with classroom lessons results in improved test scores. *Science Daily*. Retrieved from www.sciencedaily.com/releases/2011/05/110501183653.htm.

American Cancer Society. (2010). Leisure time spent sitting in relation to total mortality in a prospective cohort of U.S. adults. *American Journal of Epidemiology 172*(4), 419-429.

Brownson, R. C., T. K. Boehmer, et al. (2005). Declining rates of physical activity in the United States: What are the contributors? *Annul Review of Public Health, 26*: 421-443.

Centers for Disease Control and Prevention (CDC). (2010). Putting physical activity where it fits in the school day: Preliminary results of the ABC (Activity Bursts in the Classroom) for Fitness Program. *Preventing chronic disease: Public health research, practice, and policy* 7(4). Retrieved from http://www.cdc.gov/pcd/issues/2010/jul/pdf/09_0176.pdf.

Centers for Disease Control and Prevention (CDC). (2011a). *Adult obesity*. Retrieved from www.cdc.gov/obesity/data/adult.html.

Centers for Disease Control and Prevention (CDC). (2011b). *Data and statistics: Obesity rates among all children in the United States*. Retrieved from www.cdc.gov/obesity/childhood/data.html.

Dwyer, T., Sallis, J.F., Blizzard, L., Lazarus, R., & Dean, K. (2001). Relation of academic performance to physical activity in children. *Pediatric Exercise Science* 13:225-237.

Etnier, J. (1997). The influence of physical fitness and exercise upon cognitive functioning: A meta-analysis. *Journal of Sport and Exercise Psychology* 19, 249-277.

Hillman, C.H., Pontifex, M.B., Raine, I.B., Castelli, D.M., Hall, E.E., & Kramer, A.F. (2009). The effect of acute treadmill walking on cognitive control and academic achievement in preadolescent children. *Neuroscience* 159, 1044-1054.

Madigan, J.B. (2000). *Thinking on your feet*. Murphy, TX: Action Based Learning.

Madigan, J.B. (2006). *The action based learning lab manual*. Murphy, TX: Action Based Learning. Medina, J. (2008). *Brain rules*. WA: Pear Press.

Ratey, J. (2008). *Spark: The revolutionary new science of exercise and the brain*. New York: Little, Brown and Company.

Texas Youth Fitness Study. (March 2009). Dallas: Cooper Institute.

Villaire, T. (n.d.). *Decline of physical activity*. Retrieved from www.pta.org/topic_decline_of_physical_activity.asp

WHO Consultation on Obesity. (1999). *Obesity: Preventing and managing the global epidemic*. Retrieved from http://whqlibdoc.who.int/trs/WHO_TRS_894.pdf.

About the Author

Debby Mitchell, EdD, has over 35 years of experience in physical education, coaching, fitness, and health. Mitchell is recently retired as an associate professor at the University of Central Florida, where her research interests included brain research, developmentally appropriate movement activities and music, dance and rhythms, children's wellness, obesity, and integrating technology into the curriculum.

She founded a company called Geo-Motion Group to encourage people from all walks of life to get and remain fit. Mitchell works with schools that want to improve learning and increase physical activity. Her programs are in over 15,000 schools, and she has trained more than 800 preservice teachers and 3,000 educators at conferences in addition to writing books and delivering keynotes. In her leisure time, she enjoys being active herself through dancing, Spinning, and playing tennis.